MANAGERIAL ECONOMICS

UNDERSTANDING OF ECONOMICS' FUNDAMENTAL CONCEPTS AND ISSUES

DR. MUKTA GOYAL

Contents

Preface

Business Organizations need to go with vital choices on an everyday premise. These choices can be about a venture an open door, another item, another contender, or an organization's heading. For such significant choices, organizations need to depend on specialists. These specialists come from the foundation of Managerial Economics. Administrative Economists get to find a seat at the table with the chiefs as opposed to be a piece of the organization's presidential branch. They are the specialists who offer financial benefit to the various open doors and afterward encourage the organization to continue.

Managerial economics is a flood of the executives concentrates on that accentuates principally tackling business issues and direction by applying the hypotheses and standards of microeconomics and macroeconomics. It is a particular stream managing an association's interior issues utilizing different financial speculations. Financial aspects is an essential piece of any business. This single idea determines all the business suppositions, estimating, and speculations. This is administrative financial aspects, significance more or less.

Managerial economics is the recently presented subject in designing schooling. As of now, Text Books of Managerial Economics is intriguing in the market however this subject is fascinating and essential piece of business educational program. Notwithstanding, this course might be hard for certain understudies. Dominating the subject requirements the great comprehension of how the essential idea of financial aspects can be joined designing and the board exercises for decision making with the assistance of the instruments of arithmetic and insights. The idea and application standards has taken in due thought in this book.

The goal of this book is to grant the information on monetary standards application in designing, the board and creation for decsion making . This objective can be relized by the utilization of diagrams and tables given in the book. The utilization of the ideas or models, design makes the text more intelligible and works with advancing by permitting understudies to see administrative financial aspects can be decsion making .

This book will be useful for engineering and also engineering diploma students of various universities, it is also useful for MBA students.

I will be incredibly thankful to every one of the perusers of this course book for the valuable analysis demonstrating any mistake and oversight and so on for working on the nature of this reading material.

Dr. Mukta Goyal

Acknowledgements

I am grateful to my family members for their ongoing encouragement and cooperation during the Manuscript's preparation.

CHAPTER I

Managerial Economics-Introduction

Introduction

Managerial Economics

Managerial Economics matters is the use of financial matters to navigation. A financial aspects division overcomes any barrier between unique hypotheses and administrative practice. For recognizing issues, sorting out information, and surveying choices, it is centered around the monetary examination.

Managerial Economicsaspects is objective arranged and prescriptive ordinarily, with the vision of accomplishing ideal outcomes. In their own terms, a few business analysts and masterminds have given various meanings of administrative financial aspects.

"Managerial economics is concerned with the application of economic concepts and economic analysis to the problems of formulating rational managerial decisions."

- Edwin Mansfield, Economics Professor, University of Pennsylvania

The key of Managerial Economics is the micro-economic theory of the firm. It lessens the gap between economics in theory and economics in practice. Managerial Economics is a science dealing with effective use of scarce resources. It guides the managers in taking decisions relating to the firm's customers, competitors, suppliers as well as relating to the internal functioning of a firm. It makes use of statistical and analytical tools to assess economic theories in solving practical business problems.

Study of Managerial Economics helps in enhancement of analytical skills, assists in rational configuration as well as solution of problems. While microeconomics is the study of decisions made regarding the allocation of resources and prices of goods and services, macroeconomics is the field of economics that studies the behavior of the economy as a whole (i.e. entire industries and economies). Managerial Economics applies micro-economic tools to make business decisions. It deals with a firm.

The use of Managerial Economics is not limited to profit-making firms and organizations. But it can also be used to help in decision-making process of non-profit organizations (hospitals, educational institutions, etc). It enables optimum utilization of scarce resources in such organizations as well as helps in achieving the goals in most efficient manner. Managerial Economics is of great help in price analysis, production analysis, capital budgeting, risk analysis and determination of demand.

Managerial economics uses both Economic theory as well as Econometrics for rational managerial decision making. Econometrics is defined as use of statistical tools for assessing economic theories by empirically measuring relationship between economic variables. It uses factual data for solution of economic problems. Managerial Economics is associated with the economic theory which constitutes "Theory of Firm". Theory of firm states that the primary aim of the firm is to maximize wealth. Decision making in managerial economics generally involves establishment of firm's objectives, identification of problems involved in achievement of those objectives, development of various alternative solutions, selection of best alternative and finally implementation of the decision.

Managerial Economics strategies can be utilized to assess practically any business choice, yet they are generally broadly applied to:

Risk examination - An assortment of models are utilized to quantify risk and topsy-turvy subtleties, as well as to fuse them into risk the board choice regulations.

Creation Analysis - Microeconomic strategies are utilized to survey creation effectiveness, ideal element distribution, costs, economies of scale, and to appraise the association's expense work underway investigation.

Valuing examination - Microeconomic strategies are utilized to survey different evaluating choices including move valuing, cost separation, cost flexibility assessments, joint item estimating, and pursuing a decision of the ideal estimating strategy.

Managerial Economics can be characterized as blend of monetary hypothesis with strategic policies in order to ease direction and future preparation by the board. Administrative Economics helps the chiefs of a firm in a reasonable arrangement of snags looked in the company's exercises. It utilizes monetary hypothesis and ideas. It helps in figuring out coherent administrative choices.

The key of Managerial Economics is the miniature financial hypothesis of the firm. It reduces the hole between financial aspects in principle and financial matters practically speaking. Administrative Economics is a science managing compelling utilization of scant assets. It directs the directors in taking choices connecting with the company's clients, rivals, providers as well as connecting with the interior working of a firm. It utilizes measurable and insightful instruments to survey monetary speculations in taking care of down to earth business issues.

Investigation of Managerial Economics helps in improvement of logical abilities, aids normal design as well as arrangement of issues. While microeconomics is the investigation of choices made with respect to the allotment of assets and costs of labor and products, macroeconomics is the field of financial matters that concentrates on the way of behaving of the economy in general (for example whole ventures and economies). Administrative Economics applies miniature financial apparatuses to go with business choices. It manages a firm.

Managerial Economics involve both Economic hypotheses as well as Econometrics for judicious administrative navigation. Econometrics is characterized as utilization of factual instruments for evaluating monetary hypotheses by observationally estimating connection between financial factors. It involves verifiable information for arrangement of monetary issues. Administrative Economics is related with the monetary hypothesis which comprises the "Hypothesis of Firm". The hypothesis of firm expresses that the essential point of the firm is to expand abundance. Decision making in administrative financial aspects for the most part includes foundation of company's goals, ID of issues engaged with accomplishment of those targets, improvement of different elective arrangements, choice of best other option lastly execution of the choice.

Managerial Economics is a stream of management studies that emphasizes primarily solving business problems and decision-making by applying the theories and principles of microeconomics and macroeconomics. It is a specialized stream dealing with an organization's internal issues by using various economic theories. Economics is an indispensable part of any business. All the business assumptions, forecasting, and investments are derived from this single concept. This is managerial economics meaning in a nutshell.

Nature of Managerial Economics

The utilization of Managerial Economics isn't restricted to benefit making firms and associations. Be that as it may, it can likewise be utilized to help in dynamic course of non-benefit associations (medical clinics, instructive organizations, and so forth). It empowers ideal usage of scant assets in such associations as well as helps in accomplishing the objectives in most productive way. Administrative Economics is of extraordinary assistance in cost examination, creation investigation, capital planning, risk investigation and assurance of interest.

You need to know about its various characteristics to get more information about managerial economics. In the mentioned below points let's read about the nature of this concept:

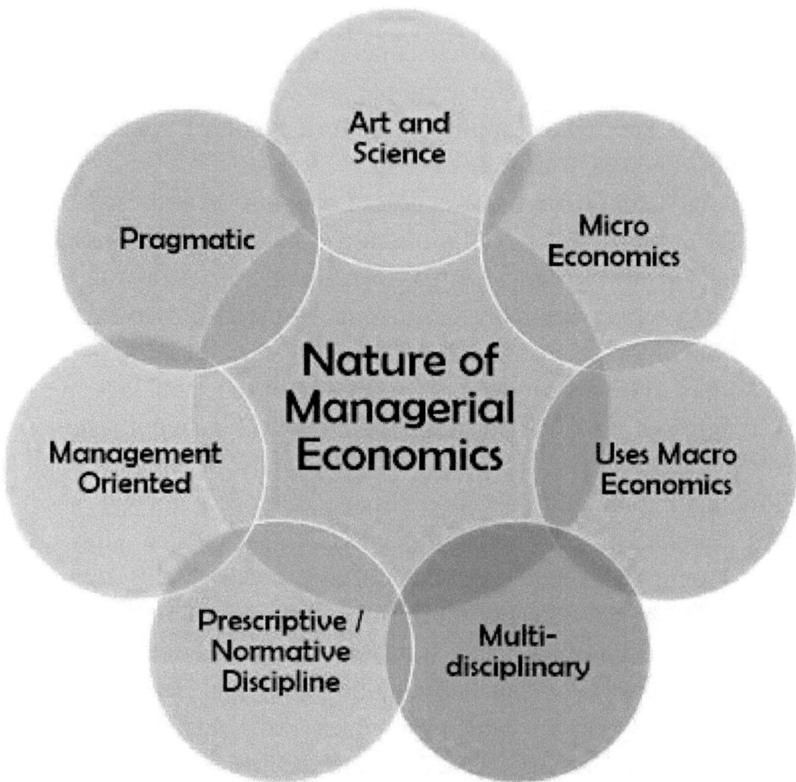

goo.gl/qnzTGNSDNNkP4thM8

1. **Art and Science**: Management theory requires a lot of critical and logical thinking and analytical skills to make decisions or solve problems. Many economists also find it a source of research, saying it includes applying different economic concepts, techniques, and methods to solve business problems.
2. **Micro Economics:** In managerial economics, managers typically deal with the problems relevant to a single entity rather than the economy as a whole.

It is therefore considered an integral part of microeconomics.

1. **Uses Macro Economics:** A corporation works in an external world, i.e. it serves the consumer, which is an important part of the economy.
2. For this purpose, it is important that managers evaluate the various macroeconomic factors such as market dynamics, economic changes, government policies, etc., and their effect on the company.
3. **Multidisciplinary:** It uses many tools and principles that belong to different disciplines, such as accounting, finance, statistics, mathematics, production, operational research, human resources, marketing, etc.
4. **Prescriptive/Normative Discipline:** By introducing corrective steps it aims at achieving the objective and solves specific issues or problems.
5. **Management Oriented:** This serves as an instrument in managers' hands to deal effectively with business-related problems and uncertainties. This also allows for setting priorities, formulating policies, and taking successful decision-making.
6. **Pragmatic:** The solution to day-to-day business challenges is realistic and rational.

Both managers take a different view of the principle of managerial economics. Others may concentrate more on customer service while others may make efficient production a priority.

Scope of Managerial Economics

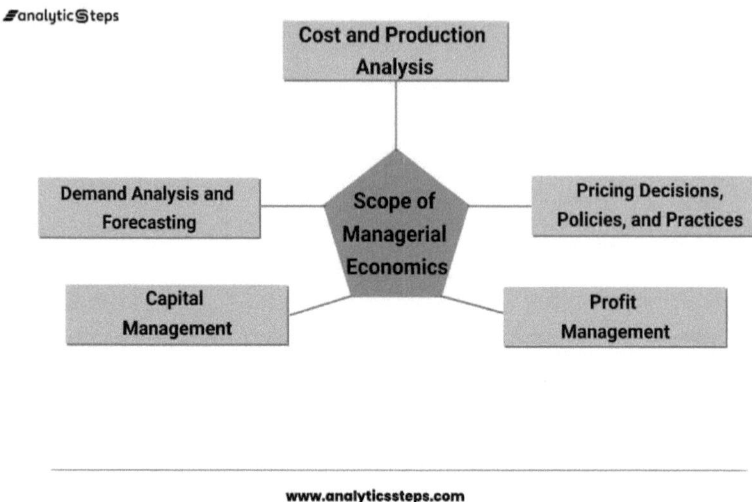

1. **Decision making:** Managerial economics helps business organizations in taking effective decisions. It tells how management can use various quantitative tools and economic theories for formulating policies and various managerial decisions.
2. **Production and cost analysis:** It helps in estimating the cost of production and determines factors causing variations in cost estimates. Managerial economics properly analyses and decides production activities and costs associated with them. It ensures that all resources are efficiently utilized which reduces the overall cost.
3. **Demand Analysis and Forecasting:** Managerial economics enables the business in analyzing demand and forecasting future uncertainties. An accurate estimate of demand will help in preparing the right production schedules and employing resources accordingly.
4. **Pricing policies:** Pricing is one of the key decisions to be taken by every business organization for earning the desired profits and attaining desired growth. Managerial economics supplies all relevant data to managers for deciding the right prices for products. Key aspects covered under this area are Pricing methods, product-line pricing, differential pricing, and price determination in various market forms.

5. **Profit management:** Managerial economics helps in managing the profit of business organizations. Profit is the main measure for the success or growth of firm in the long run. It helps in making correct estimates of all cost and revenue at different levels of outputs which helps in earning the desired profit.
6. **Capital management:** Capital investment decisions is one of the most challenging and complex tasks before every manager. Managerial economics helps in planning and managing all capital expenditures of business which requires huge investment. It properly analyses investment avenues before investing any amount into it to ensure the profitability of an investment.

Significance of Managerial Economics

1. **Business Planning:** Managerial economics assists business organizations in formulating plans and better decision making. It helps in analyzing the demand and forecasting future business activities.

2.**Cost Control:**Controlling the cost is another important role played by managerial economics. It properly analyses and decides production activities and the cost associated with them. Managerial economics ensure that all resources are efficiently utilized which reduces the overall cost.

3.**Price Determination:** Setting the right price is one of the key decisions to be taken by every business organization. Managerial economics supplies all relevant data to managers for deciding the right prices for products.

4.**Business Prediction:** Managerial economics through the application of various economic tools and theories helps managers in predicting various future uncertainties. Timely detection of uncertainties helps in taking all possible steps to avoid them.

5.**Profit Planning And Control:** Managerial economics enables in planning and managing the profit of the business. It makes an accurate estimate of all cost and revenue which helps in earning the desired profit.

6.**Inventory Management:** Proper management of inventory is a must for ensuring the continuity of business activities. It helps in analyzing the demand and accordingly, production activities are performed. Managers can arrange and ensure that the proper quantity of inventory is always available within the business organization.

7.**Manages Capital:** Managerial economics helps in taking all decisions relating to the firm's capital. It properly analyses investment avenues before investing any amount into it to ensure the profitability of an investment.

Managerial Eonomics Relationship with other disciplines

Many new subjects have evolved in recent years due to the interaction among basic disciplines. While there are many such new subjects in natural and social sciences, managerial economics can be taken as the best example of such a phenomenon among social sciences. Hence it is necessary to trace its roots and relationship with other disciplines.

1. Relationship with economics

The relationship between managerial economics and economics theory may be viewed form the point of view of the two approaches to the subject Viz. Micro Economics and Marco Economics. Microeconomics is the study of the economic behavior of individuals, firms and other such micro organizations. Managerial economics is rooted in Micro Economic theory. Managerial Economics makes use to several Micro Economic concepts such as marginal cost, marginal revenue, elasticity of demand as well as price theory and theories of market structure to name only a few. Macro theory on the other hand is the study of the economy as a whole. It deals with the analysis of national income, the level of employment, general price level, consumption and investment in the economy and even matters related to international trade, Money, public finance, etc.

2. Management theory and accounting

Managerial economics has been influenced by developments in management theory and accounting techniques. Accounting refers to the recording of pecuniary transactions of the firm in certain books. A proper knowledge of accounting techniques is very essential for the success of the firm because profit maximization is the major objective of the firm.

Managerial Economics requires a proper knowledge of cost and revenue information and their classification. A student of managerial economics should be familiar with the generation, interpretation and use of accounting data. The focus of accounting within the firm is fast changing from the concepts of store keeping to that if managerial decision making, this has resulted in a new specialized area of study called “Managerial Accounting”.

3. Managerial Economics and mathematics

The use of mathematics is significant for managerial economics in view of its profit maximization goal long with optional use of resources. The major problem of the firm is how to minimize cost, hoe to maximize profit or how to optimize sales. Mathematical concepts and techniques are widely used in economic logic to solve these problems. Also mathematical methods help to estimate and predict the economic factors for decision making and forward planning.

4. Managerial Economics and Statistics

Managerial Economics needs the tools of statistics in more than one way. A successful businessman must correctly estimate the demand for his product. He should be able to analyses the impact of variations in tastes. Fashion and changes in income on demand only then he can adjust his output. Statistical methods provide and sure base for decision-making. Thus statistical tools are used in collecting data and analyzing them to help in the decision making process.

5. Managerial Economics and Operations Research

Taking effective decisions is the major concern of both managerial economics and operations research. The development of techniques and concepts such as linear programming, inventory models and game theory is due to the development of this new subject of operations research in the postwar years. Operations research is concerned with the complex problems arising out of the management of men, machines, materials and money.

6. Managerial Economics and the theory of Decision- making

The Theory of decision-making is a new field of knowledge grown in the second half of this century. Most of the economic theories explain a single goal for the consumer i.e., Profit maximization for the firm. But the theory of decision-making is developed to explain multiplicity of goals and lot of uncertainty.

7. Managerial Economics and Computer Science

Computers have changes the way of the world functions and economic or business activity is no exception. Computers are used in data and accounts maintenance, inventory and stock controls and supply and demand predictions. What used to take days and months is done in a few minutes or hours by the computers. In fact computerization of business activities on a large scale has reduced the workload of managerial personnel. In most countries a basic knowledge of computer science, is a compulsory programme for managerial trainees.

A successful managerial economist must be a mathematician, a statistician and an economist. He must be also able to combine philosophic methods with historical methods to get the right perspective only then; he will be good at predictions. In short managerial practices with the help of other allied sciences.

Role of Managerial Economics in Decision Making

1. **Studies Business Environment:** Managerial economics properly analyze the external environment within which the business operates. These factors influence the working of the business and therefore should be considered while taking any decisions and framing policies. Managerial economic studies all factors like economic scenario, government policies, price trends, national income growth, etc.
2. **.Production Scheduling:** Managerial economics manages and prepare schedules for all production activities of business. It estimates all future demands using various quantitative tools which helps in making production plans.
3. **Control Cost:** Controlling the cost is vital for achieving the desired profitability and growth. Managerial economics estimates the cost of all business activities and identify all those factors that cause variations in cost from time to time. It aims at minimizing the cost through optimum utilization of all resources.
4. **Set Prices:** Setting the right price is a very challenging task for every business organization. Managerial economics helps management in fixing the correct price by supplying all information regarding competitors pricing methods.
5. **Bring Coordination:** Managerial economics brings coordination and flexibility in all operations of the business. It supports effective decision making by providing all relevant data using economic theories and tools.
6. **Investment Analysis:** Managerial economics ensures that all business funds are allocated to profitable means. It properly analyzes the profitability of all investment avenues before investing any amount into them.

Principle Of Managerial Economics

Managerial Economics is both conceptual and metrical. Before the substantive decision problems which fall within the purview of managerial economics are discussed, it is useful to identify and understand some of the basic concepts underlying the subject.

Therefore, it would be useful to examine the basic tools of managerial economics and the nature and extent of gap between the economic theory of the firm and the managerial theory of the firm. The contribution of economics to managerial economics lies in certain principles which are basic to managerial economics. **There are six basic principles of managerial economics.**

They are:-

1. The Incremental Principle

The incremental concept is probably the most important concept in economics and is certainly the most frequently used in Managerial Economics. The incremental concept is closely related to the marginal cost and marginal revenues of economic theory.

The two major concepts in this analysis are incremental cost and incremental revenue. The incremental cost denotes a change in total cost, whereas incremental revenue means a change in total revenue resulting from a decision of the firm.

The incremental principle may be stated as follows:

A decision is clearly a profitable one if

i. It increases revenue more than costs.
ii. It decreases some cost to a greater extent than it increases others.
iii. It increases some revenues more than it decreases others.
iv. It reduces costs more than revenues.

2. Marginal Principle

Marginal analysis implies judging the impact of a unit change in one variable on the other. Marginal generally refers to small changes. Marginal revenue is change in total revenue per unit change in output sold. Marginal cost refers to change in total costs per unit change in output produced (While incremental cost refers to change in total costs due to change in total output). The decision of a firm to change the price would depend upon the resulting impact/change in marginal revenue and marginal cost. If the marginal revenue is greater than the marginal cost, then the firm should bring about the change in price.

3. The Opportunity Cost Principle

Both micro and macro economics make abundant use of the fundamental concept of opportunity cost. In everyday life, we apply the notion of opportunity cost even if we are unable to articulate its significance. In Managerial Economics, the opportunity cost concept is useful in decision involving a choice between different alternative courses of action.

Opportunity cost of a decision is the sacrifice of alternatives required by that decision. Sacrifice of alternatives is involved when carrying out a decision requires using a resource that is limited in supply with the firm. Opportunity cost, therefore, represents the benefits or revenue forgone by pursuing one course of action rather than another.

The concept of opportunity cost implies three things:

i. The calculation of opportunity cost involves the measurement of sacrifices.
ii. Sacrifices may be monetary or real.
iii. The opportunity cost is termed as the cost of sacrificed alternatives.

In managerial decision making, the concept of opportunity cost occupies an important place. The economic significance of opportunity cost is as follows:

i. It helps in determining relative prices of different goods.
ii. It helps in determining normal remuneration to a factor of production.
iii. It helps in proper allocation of factor resources.

4. Discounting Principle

This concept is an extension of the concept of time perspective. Since future is unknown and incalculable, there is lot of risk and uncertainty in future. Everyone knows that a rupee today is worth more than a rupee will be two years from now. This appears similar to the saying that "a bird in hand is more worth than two in the bush." This judgment is made not on account of the uncertainty surrounding the future or the risk of inflation.

5. Concept of Time Perspective

The time perspective concept states that the decision maker must give due consideration both to the short run and long run effects of his decisions. He must give due emphasis to the various time periods. It was Marshall who introduced time element in economic theory.

The economic concepts of the long run and the short run have become part of everyday language. Managerial economists are also concerned with the short run and long run effects of decisions on revenues as well as costs. The main problem in decision making is to establish the right balance between long run and short run.

In the short period, the average cost of a firm may be either more or less than its average revenue. In the long period, the average cost of the firm will be equal to its average revenue. A decision may be made on the basis of short run considerations, but may as time elapses have long run repercussions which make it more or less profitable than it at first appeared.

6. Equi-Marginal Principle

One of the widest known principles of economics is the equi-marginal principle. The principle states that an input should be allocated so that value added by the last unit is the same in all cases. This generalization is popularly called the equi-marginal.

Let us assume a case in which the firm has 100 unit of labour at its disposal. And the firm is involved in five activities viz., A, B, C, D and E. The firm can increase any one of these activities by employing more labour but only at the cost i.e., sacrifice of other activities.

An optimum allocation cannot be achieved if the value of the marginal product is greater in one activity than in another. It would be, therefore, profitable to shift labour from low marginal value activity to high marginal value activity, thus increasing the total value of all products taken together.

Production Possibility Curve

An economy's factors of production are scarce; they cannot produce an unlimited quantity of goods and services. A production possibilities curve is a graphical representation of the alternative combinations of goods and services an economy can produce. It illustrates the production possibilities model. In drawing the production possibilities curve, we shall assume that the economy can produce only two goods and that the quantities of factors of production and the technology available to the economy are fixed.

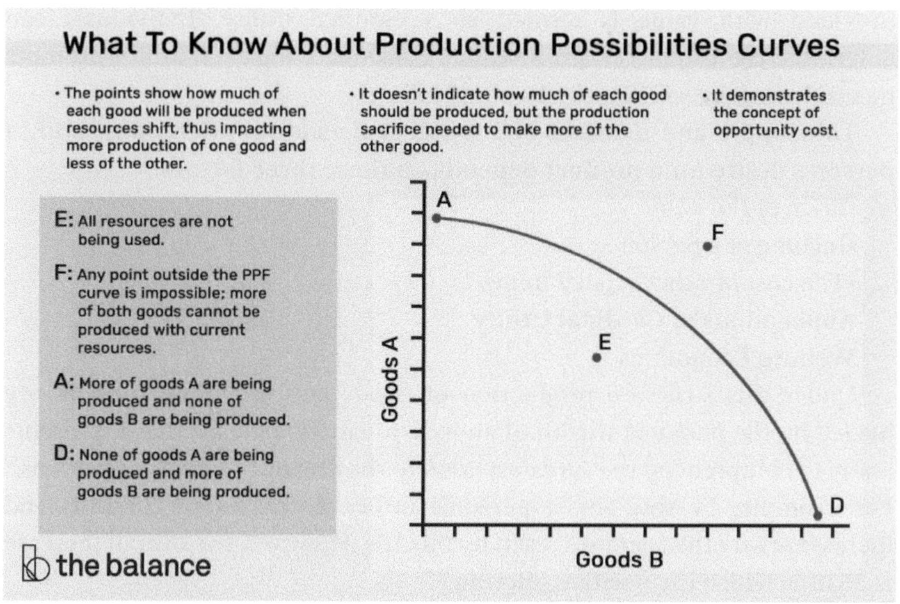

thebalance.com

The Opportunity cost of producing more manufactured goods is increasing as we give up increasing amounts of agricultural products to achieve it.

The reason is that different factors of production have different properties or skills and as we concentrate more and more on the production of one thing we have to start using resources that are less and less suitable for it.

Cardinal And Ordinal Approaches To Consumer Behaviour

Utility is a psychological phenomenon; that implies the satisfying power of a good or service. It differs from person to person, as it depends on a person's mental attitude. The measurability of utility is always a matter of contention.

The two principal theories for utility are cardinal utility and ordinal utility. Many traditional economists hold the view that utility is measured quantitatively, like length, height, weight, temperature, etc. This concept is known as the cardinal utility concept.

What is Cardinal Utility?

The proposition that economic prosperity can be rightly perceived and provided with value is termed as a cardinal utility. Individuals can determine the use of certain products consumed. Cardinal utility prompts measuring of the satisfactory levels in utils.

The supply and demand of a product decide its price. Moreover, a person's desire for a product depends on these three factors:

•Price of the item

•Income of a person

•The cost of other related items

Applications of Cardinal Utility

Welfare Economics

Under this structure production of goods and providing services are judged by the personal wealth of an individual. This means that it presents a way to comprehend the "greatest good to the greatest number of persons". For example, by this act, a person's utility decreases by 75 utils and increases two other persons' each by 50 utils. However, the overall increase is 25 utils which is a positive offering.

Marginalism

In cardinal theory, a product's marginal utility sign is alike for all the mathematical forms, but its magnitude is not same. This applies for second derivative of a differentiable utility as well.

Expected Utility Theory

This framework works for settlements that are to made under risks. Suppose there are a few lottery tickets that will provide outcomes. Here, it is possible to plot preferences in real numbers so that numerical representation can be done.

Intertemporal Utility

In various representations of utility, where people deduct the upcoming values of utility, cardinality comes into play. With the use of this, it is feasible to generate proper utility functions.

What is Ordinal Utility?

Ordinal Utility is propounded by the modern economists, J.R. Hicks, and R.G.D. Allen, which states that it is not possible for consumers to express the satisfaction derived from a commodity in absolute or numerical terms. Modern Economists hold that utility being a psychological phenomenon, cannot be measured quantitatively, theoretically and conceptually. However, a person can introspectively express whether a good or service provides more, less or equal satisfaction when compared to one another.

In this way, the measurement of utility is ordinal, i.e. qualitative, based on the ranking of preferences for commodities. For example: Suppose a person prefers tea to coffee and coffee to milk. Hence, he or she can tell subjectively, his/her preferences, i.e. tea > coffee > milk.

Differences Between Cardinal And Ordinal Utility

The following points are noteworthy so far as the difference between cardinal and ordinal utility is concerned:

1. Cardinal utility is the utility wherein the satisfaction derived by the consumers from the consumption of good or service can be measured numerically. Ordinal utility states that the satisfaction which a consumer derives from the consumption of product or service cannot be measured numerically.
2. Cardinal utility measures the utility objectively, whereas there is a subjective measurement of ordinal utility.
3. Cardinal utility is less realistic, as quantitative measurement of utility is not possible. On the other end, the ordinal utility is more realistic as it

relies on qualitative measurement.

4. Cardinal utility, is based on marginal utility analysis. As against this, the concept of ordinal utility is based on indifference curve analysis.
5. The cardinal utility is measured in terms of utils, i.e. units of utility. On the contrary, the ordinal utility is measured in terms of ranking of preferences of a commodity when compared to each other.
6. Cardinal utility approach propounded by Alfred Marshall and his followers. Conversely, ordinal utility approach pioneered by Hicks and Allen.

Equi-Marginal Principle

The equi-marginal principle is one of the widely used concepts in managerial economics. This principle is also known the principle of maximum satisfaction - by allocating available resources to get optimum benefit .The law of equi-marginal utility tells us the way how a person maximizes his total utility.

Certain aspects of the equi-marginal principle need clarifications, which are as follows:

First, the values of marginal products are net of incremental costs. In activity B, we may add one unit of labor with an increase in physical output of 100 units. Each unit is worth 50 cents so that the 100 units will sell for 50$. But the increased output consumes raw materials, fuel and other inputs so that variable costs in activity B (not counting the labor cost) are higher. Let us say that the incremental costs are 30$ leaving a net addition of 20$. The value of the marginal product relevant for our purpose is thus 20$.

Secondly, if the revenues resulting from the addition of labor are to occur in future, these revenues should be discounted before comparisons in the alternative activities are possible. Activity A may produce revenue immediately but activities B, C and D may take 2, 3 and 5 years respectively. Here the discounting of these revenues will make them equivalent.

Thirdly, the measurement of value of the marginal product may have to be corrected if the expansion of an activity requires an alternative reduction in the prices of the output. If activity B represents the production of radios and it is not possible to sell more radios without a reduction in price, it is necessary to make adjustment for the fall in price.

Fourthly, the equi-marginal principle may break under sociological pressures. For instance, due to inertia, activities are continued simply because they exist. Similarly, due to their empire building ambitions, managers may keep on expanding activities to fulfill their desire for power. Departments, which are already over-budgeted often, use some of their excess resources to build up propaganda machines (public relations offices) to win additional support. Governmental agencies are more prone to bureaucratic self-perpetuation and inertia.

Law of Diminishing Marginal Utility

The Law of Diminishing Marginal Utility states that, all else equal, as consumption increases, the marginal utility derived from each additional unit declines. Marginal utility is derived as the change inutilityas an additional unit is consumed. Utility is an economic term used to represent satisfaction or happiness. Marginal utility is the incremental increase in utility that results from the consumption of one additional unit.

Understanding the Law of Diminishing Marginal Utility

Whenever an individual interacts or consumes an economic good, that individual acts in a way that demonstrates the order in which they value the use of that good. Thus, the first unit that is consumed satisfies the consumers' greatest need. The second unit satisfies results in a lesser amount of satisfaction. and so on.

The Law and Marketing

Marketers use the law of diminishing marginal utility because they want to keep marginal utility high for products that they sell. A product is consumed because it provides satisfaction, but too much of a product might mean that the marginal utility reaches zero because consumers have had enough of a product and are satiated. Of course, marginal utility depends on the consumer and the product being consumed.

Indifference Curve Analysis

An indifference curve, with respect to two commodities, is a graph showing those combinations of the two commodities that leave the consumer equally well off or equally satisfied—hence indifferent—in having any combination on the curve.

Indifference curves are heuristic devices used in contemporary microeconomics to demonstrate consumer preference and the limitations of a budget. Economists have adopted the principles of indifference curves in the study of welfare economics.

Properties of Indifference Curves

If a good satisfies all four properties of indifference curves, the goods are referred to as ordinary goods. They can be summarized as the consumer requires more of one good to compensate for less consumption of another good, and the consumer experiences a diminishing marginal rate of substitution when deciding between two goods.

1. **Indifference curves never cross.** If they could cross, it would create large amounts of ambiguity as to what the true utility is.
2. **The farther out an indifference curve lies, the farther it is from the origin, and the higher the level of utility it indicates.** As illustrated above on the indifference curve map, the farther out from the origin, the more utility the individual generates while consuming.
3. **Indifference curves slope downwards.** The only way an individual can increase consumption in one good without gaining utility is to consume another good and generate the same amount of utility. Therefore, the slope is downwards sloping.
4. **Indifference curves assume a convex shape.** As illustrated above in the indifference curve map, the curve gets flatter as you move down the curve to the right. It illustrates that all individuals experience diminishing marginal utility, where additional consumption of another good will generate a lesser amount of utility than the prior.

Hence,An indifference curve is a contour line where utility remains constant across all points on the line. In economics, an indifference curve is a line drawn between different consumption bundles, on a graph charting the quantity of good A consumed versus the quantity of good B consumed. At each of the consumption bundles, the individual is said to be indifferent.

CHAPTER II

Introduction to Macro Economics

Introduction

Macroeconomics is a branch of economics that studies how an overall economy—the market or other systems that operate on a large scale—behaves. Macroeconomics studies economy-wide phenomena such as inflation, price levels, rate of economic growth, national income, gross domestic product (GDP), and changes in unemployment.

Some of the key questions addressed by macroeconomics include: What causes unemployment? What causes inflation? What creates or stimulates economic growth? Macroeconomics attempts to measure how well an economy is performing, to understand what forces drive it, and to project how performance can improve.

Macroeconomics deals with the performance, structure, and behavior of the entire economy, in contrast to microeconomics, which is more focused on the choices made by individual actors in the economy (like people, households, industries, etc.

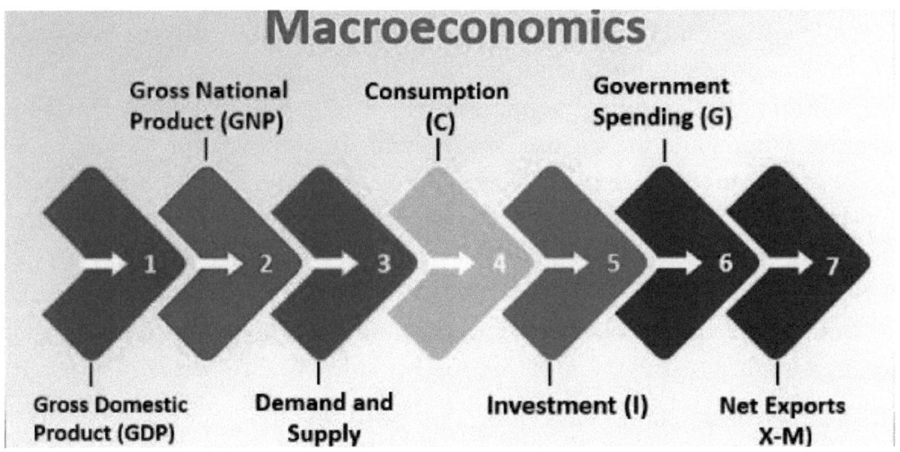

proprofs.com

Nature of Macroeconomics

The term ‘macro’ was first used in economics by Ragner Frisch in 1933. But as a methodological approach to economic problems, it originated with the Mercantilists in the 16th and 17th centuries. They were concerned with the economic system as a whole.Macroeconomics is basically known as the theory of income. It is concerned with the problems of economic fluctuations, unemployment, inflation or deflation, and economic growth. It deals with the aggregates of all quantities not with individual price levels or outputs but with national output.

Macroeconomics is the study of aggregates or averages covering the entire economy, such as total employment, national income, national output, total investment, total consumption, total savings, aggregate supply, aggregate demand, and general price level, wage level, and cost structure.

In other words, it is aggregative economics which examines the interrelations among the various aggregates, their determination and causes of fluctuations in them. Thus in the words of Professor Ackley, “Macroeconomics deals with economic affairs in the large, it concerns the overall dimensions of economic life. It looks at the total size and shape and functioning of the “elephant” of economic experience, rather than working of articulation or dimensions of the individual parts. It studies the character of the forest, independently of the trees which compose it.”

Macroeconomics is also known as the theory of income and employment, or simply income analysis. It is concerned with the problems of unemployment, economic fluctuations, inflation or deflation, international trade and economic growth. It is the study of the causes of unemployment, and the various determinants of employment.

In the field of business cycles, it concerns itself with the effect of investment on total output, total income, and aggregate employment. In the monetary sphere, it studies the effect of the total quantity of money on the general price level.

Both microeconomics and macroeconomics involve the study of aggregates. But aggregation in microeconomics is different from that in macroeconomics. In microeconomics the interrelationships of individual households, individual firms and individual industries to each other deal with aggregation.

“The concept of ‘industry’, for example, aggregates numerous firms or even products. Consumer demand for shoes is an aggregate of the demands of many households, and the supply of shoes is an aggregate of the production of many firms.

The demand and supply of labour in a locality are clearly aggregate concepts." "However, the aggregates of microeconomic theory," according to Professor Bilas, "do not deal with the behaviour of the billions of dollars of consumer expenditures, business investments, and government expenditures. These are in the realm of microeconomics."

The front-side of macroeconomics is microeconomics. Microeconomics is the investigation of the financial activities of people and little gatherings of people. The "investigation of specific firms, specific families, individual costs, compensation, earnings, individual enterprises, specific wares." But macroeconomics "manages totals of these amounts; not with individual livelihoods but rather with the public pay, not with individual costs but rather with the cost levels, not with individual result but rather with the public result."

Microeconomics, as per Ackley, "manages the division of all out yield among businesses, items, and firms, and the assignment of assets among contending utilizes. It thinks about issues of pay dispersion. Its advantage is in relative costs of specific labor and products."

Macroeconomics, then again, "worries about such factors as the total volume of the result of an economy, with the degree to which its assets are utilized, with the size of the public pay, with the 'general cost level'."

Thus the scope of microeconomics to aggregates relates to the economy as a whole, "together with sub-aggregates which (a) cross product and industry lines (such as the total production of consumer goods, or total production of capital goods), and which (b) add up to an aggregate for the whole economy (as total production of consumer goods and of capital goods add up to total production of the economy; or as total wage income and property income add up to national income)." Thus microeconomics uses aggregates relating to individual households, firms and industries, while macroeconomics uses aggregates which relate them to the "economy wide total".

As per G. Ackley, Macroeconomics concerns itself with such variables –

- The aggregate volume of the output of an economy.
- The extent to which resources are employed.
- Size of the national income.
- General price level.

Importance of Macroeconomics

1. **Functioning of an Economy:-** Macroeconomics analysis is of paramount importance in getting us an idea of the functioning of an economic system. It is very essential for a proper and accurate knowledge of the behaviour pattern of the aggregative variables as the description of a large and complex economic system is impossible in terms of numerous individual items.
2. **Formulation of Economic Policies:-** Macroeconomic is of great help in the formulation of economic policies. The days of 'laissez faire' are over and government intervention in economic matters is an accomplished fact. Governments deal not with the individuals, thereby establishing the importance of studies. For example, during depression, when the machines lie idle and men roam from pillar to post in search of employment, macroeconomics helps us to analyse the cause leading to depression and employment and to the adoption of suitable policies to cope with such a situation.
3. **Understanding Macroeconomics:-** The study of macroeconomics is essential for the proper understanding of microeconomics. No microeconomics law could be framed without a prior study of aggregates; for example:- the theory of individual firm could not have been formulated with reference to the behaviour pattern of one single firm, howsoever representative it might have been; the theory was possible only after the behaviour pattern of several firms had been examined and analyzed, for example, the forest, though an aggregation of trees, does not exhibit the behaviour and characteristics of individual trees. Microeconomics has been, and to some extent, remains a jungle of special assumptions, special cases, unsatisfactory measurements and abstract theorising.
4. **Understanding and Controlling Economic Fluctuations:-**Economic fluctuations are a characteristic feature of the capitalist form of society. The theory of economic fluctuations can be understood and built up only with the help of macroeconomics, for here we have to take into consideration aggregate consumption, aggregate saving and investment in the economy. Thus, we are led to analyse the causes of fluctuations in income, output and employment, and make attempts to control them or at least to reduce their severity.
5. **Inflation and Deflation:-** Macroeconomic approach is of utmost importance to analyse and understand the effects of inflation and deflation. Different sections of society are affected differently as a result

of changes in the value of money. Macroeconomic analysis enables us to take certain steps to counteract the adverse influences of inflation and deflation.

6. **Study of National Income:-** It is the study of macroeconomics which has brought forward the immerse importance of the study of national income and social accounts. In micro economy such a study was relegated to the background. It is the study of national income which enables us to know that three fourth of the world is living in abject poverty. Without a study of national income, as a result of the development in macroeconomics, it was not possible to formulate correct economic policies.

What is economic growth

A country's general economic health can be measured by looking at that country's economic growth and development. Let's take a separate look at what indicators comprise economic growth versus economic development.

Let's first examine economic growth. A country's economic growth is usually indicated by an increase in that country's gross domestic product, or GDP. Generally speaking, gross domestic product is an economic model that reflects the value of a country's output. In other words, a country's GDP is the total monetary value of the goods and services produced by that country over a specific period of time.

Examples of Economic Growth

For example, let say that a special berry grows naturally only in the country of Utopia. Natives to Utopia have used this berry for many years, but recently, a wealthyGerman traveller discovered the berry and brought samples back to Germany. His German friends also loved the berry, so the traveller funded a large berry exporting business in Utopia. The new berry exporting business hired hundreds of Utopians to farm, harvest, wash, box and ship the berries to grocers in Germany.

In one calendar year, the berry exporting business added over one million dollars to Utopia's GDP because that's the total value of the goods and services produced by the new berry exporting business. Since Utopia's GDP increased, this means that Utopia experienced economic growth.

In the United States, our periods of large economic growth are mostly associated with new technology. The Industrial Revolution and the development of the Internet are two examples. When new developments bring an increase in output capacity, economic growth usually follows.

What is Economic Development

Now let's take a look at economic development. A country's economic development is usually indicated by an increase in citizens quality of life. 'Quality of life is other measured using the Human Development Index, which is an economic model that considered intrinisic personal factors not considered in economic growth, such as literacy rates, life expectancy and poverty rates.

While economic growth often leads to economic development, it is important to note that a country's GDP doesn't include intrinisic development factors, such as leisure time, environmental quality or freedom from oppression. Using the Human Development Index, factors like literacy rates and life expectancy generally imply a higher per capita income and therefore indicate economic development.

Economic Development is projects, approaches or exercises that look to further develop the monetary prosperity and personal satisfaction for a local area.

In the economic aspects investigation of the public area, economic and social advancement is the cycle by which the economic prosperity and personal satisfaction of a country, district, neighborhood local area, or an individual are worked on as indicated by designated objectives and goals.

The term has been utilized often in the twentieth and 21st hundreds of years, yet the idea has existed in the West for far longer. "Modernization", "Westernization", and particularly "industrialization" are different terms frequently utilized while examining monetary turn of events. By and large, economic advancement arrangements zeroed in on industrialization and framework, however since the 1960s, it has progressively centered around neediness reductiion.

Though economic development is a strategy intercession intending to further develop the prosperity of individuals, economic development is a peculiarity of market efficiency and expansions in GDP; business analyst Amartya Sen portrays economic development as yet "one part of the course of monetary turn of events". Economists essentially center around the development viewpoint and the economy at large, whereas scientists of local area economic development worry about financial improvement also.

What "economic development" signifies to you will rely upon the local area you live in. Every people group has its own chances, difficulties, and needs. Your economic development arranging should incorporate individuals who live and work locally.

Economic Development Strategies

However economic development needs differ, economic development systems frequently hold back nothing, results, for example

- Making more positions and more work assortment
- Keeping organizations and getting new ones
- A superior personal satisfaction
- More individuals and organizations making good on charges
- More useful utilization of property
- Advancing your local area's resources
- Making and selling more neighborhood items
- Getting more talented laborers living locally
- Who is Responsible for Economic Development work?

Many individuals accomplishing financial improvement work are monetary advancement professionals or Economic Development Officers or "EDOs" for short. Certain individuals don't hold the authority title in their work, yet are accomplishing financial advancement work constantly.

What is an Economic Development Practitioner?

Just like economic development is different for communities, so are the economic development practitioners that support them. Generally, an economic development practitioner:

1. Plans, designs, and delivers economic development strategies.
2. Acts as an important connection between public and private sectors and the community.
3. Takes part in economic development planning and sometimes leads or gives input into the policy-making process.
4. Administers policy, programs, and projects.

Who is Responsible for Economic Development work?

Many people doing economic development work are economic development practitioners or Economic Development Officers or "EDOs" for short. Some people don't hold the official title in their job, but are doing economic development work all the time.

1. Lots of different groups can work in economic development, including:
2. Local Indigenous and non-Indigenous governments

3. Chambers of commerce
4. Technology or business incubators
5. Regional development agencies
6. Community colleges, universities and research institutions
7. Provincial and Federal governments
8. Special authorities (like airports, ports, etc.)
9. Not-for-profits & humanitarian organizations
10. Business and industry associations
11. Workforce development organizations
12. Neighbourhood groups
13. Utilities providers (help with business attraction and growth)

Their role in a community can include:

1. Leading economic development planning
2. Working toward the community's mandate or vision for economic development
3. Supporting sector relationships
4. Communicating and responding to economic development concerns and opportunities
5. Leading projects to enhance economic development
6. Providing accountability, ensuring economic development isn't an afterthought.

Start with an economic development plan and get feedback and approval. Once community support and partnerships are in place you are ready to get started.

Examples of Economic Development

For example, before the berry exporting business, most Utopians lived in small villages many miles from one another. Few Utopians had access to schools, fresh water or healthcare. Utopian men worked long hours attempting to farm land that was naturally unsuitable for most crops, just to feed their immediate families.

Methods of Measurement of National Income

The national income of a country can be measured by three alternative methods: (i) Product Method (ii) Income Method, and (iii) Expenditure Method.

1. Product Method: In this method, national income is measured as a flow of goods and services. We calculate money value of all final goods and services produced in an economy during a year. Final goods here refer to those goods which are directly consumed and not used in further production process. Goods which are further used in production process are called intermediate goods. In the value of final goods, value of intermediate goods is already included therefore we do not count value of intermediate goods in national income otherwise there will be double counting of value of goods.

To avoid the problem of double counting we can use the value-addition method in which not the whole value of a commodity but value-addition (i.e. value of final good value of intermediate good) at each stage of production is calculated and these are summed up to arrive at GDP.

The money value is calculated at market prices so sum-total is the GDP at market prices. GDP at market price can be converted into by methods discussed earlier.

2. Income Method: Under this method, national income is measured as a flow of factor incomes. There are generally four factors of production labour, capital, land and entrepreneurship. Labour gets wages and salaries, capital gets interest, land gets rent and entrepreneurship gets profit as their remuneration.

Besides, there are some self-employed persons who employ their own labour and capital such as doctors, advocates, CAs, etc. Their income is called mixed income. The sum-total of all these factor incomes is called NDP at factor costs.

3. Expenditure Method: In this method, national income is measured as a flow of expenditure. GDP is sum-total of private consumption expenditure. Government consumption expenditure, gross capital formation (Government and private) and net exports (Export-Import).

Meaning of Inflation

Inflation refers to the rise in the prices of most goods and services of daily or common use, such as food, clothing, housing, recreation, transport, consumer staples, etc. Inflation measures the average price change in a basket of commodities and services over time. The opposite and rare fall in the price index of this basket of items is called 'deflation'. Inflation is indicative of the decrease in the purchasing power of a unit of a country's currency. This is measured in percentage.

What are the effects of Inflation

The purchasing power of a currency unit decreases as the commodities and services get dearer. This also impacts the cost of living in a country. When inflation is high, the cost of living gets higher as well, which ultimately leads to a deceleration in economic growth. A certain level of inflation is required in the economy to ensure that expenditure is promoted and hoarding money through savings is demotivated.

How is inflation measured

In India, inflation is primarily measured by two main indices — WPI (Wholesale Price Index) and CPI (Consumer Price Index), which measure wholesale and retail-level price changes, respectively. The CPI calculates the difference in the price of commodities and services such as food, medical care, education, electronics etc, which Indian consumers buy for use.

On the other hand, the goods or services sold by businesses to smaller businesses for selling further is captured by the WPI. In India, both WPI (Wholesale Price Index) and CPI (Consumer Price Index) are used to measure inflation.

What are the main causes of Inflation?

The main causes of inflation in India have been subject to considerable debates and discussions. These are some of the chief reasons for the increase in prices:

- High demand and low production or supply of multiple commodities create a demand-supply gap, which leads to a hike in prices.
- Excess circulation of money leads to inflation as money loses its purchasing power.
- With people having more money, they also tend to spend more, which causes increased demand.

Theories of Inflation

1. The Demand-Pull Inflation: The theory of demand-pull inflation relates to what may be called the traditional theory of inflation.

The essence of this theory is that inflation is caused by an excess of demand (spending) relative to the available supply of goods and services at existing prices. According to classicals, the key factor is the money supply because in accordance with the quantity theory of money only an increase in the money supply is capable of raising the general price level.

In modern income theory, however, demand-pull is interpreted to mean an excess of aggregate money demand relative to the economy's full employment output level. The theory assumes that prices for goods and services as well as for economic resources are responsive to supply and demand forces, and will, thus, moves readily upward under the pressure of a high level of aggregate demand.

Economists like Friedman, Hawtrey, Golden Weiser, who regard inflation as a purely monetary phenomenon, strongly support this theory of inflation caused by excess money supply. The excess demand in the economy develops owing to large-scale investment expenditure either in the public or in the private sector, thereby exceeding the total output.

As a result of this excess demand, prices will rise and excess demand inflation or demand-pull inflation comes to exist. Thus, we find that according to this theory of demand-pull inflation, prices rise in response to an excess of aggregate demand over existing supply of goods and services caused by an increase in the quantity of money—resulting in a fall of interest rates—increasing investment expenditures and prices. But demand-pull inflation may also be caused without an increase in money supply—when MEC or MPC goes up causing an increase in expenditures and hence prices. Since inflation is due to excess demand, it is considered controllable by the demand reducing monetary and fiscal policies. The Figure 32.5 shows that pure-demand-inflation theorists tend to assume that at some income level Y_0 in the Figure corresponding to full-employment, the aggregate supply function becomes completely inelastic, as drawn. No income level lower than Y_0 is a full-employment one, and increases in demand beyond D_0, to D_1 and D_2 raise the price level from P_0 to P_1 and P_2.

Consider the diagram 32.6, which analyses the working of excess demand inflation irrespective of the fact whether excess demand is caused by increased money supply or by expenditures on C and I. Fig. 32.6

Let us suppose that the full-employment level of output remains fixed at Y_0. General equilibrium is established at Y_0 and i_0 with price level p_0. An increase in the price level may now come about as a result of an increase in aggregate demand, which shifts the IS_0 schedule to IS_1; the resulting excess demand of $Y_1 - Y_0$ leads to a bidding up prices so that the real value of the money supply shrinks and the LMp_0 schedule shifts to LMp_1, where general equilibrium is again established at the higher interest rate i_1 and higher price level p_1.

2. Cost-Push Inflation: The theory of cost-push inflation became popular during and after the Second World War. This theory maintains that prices instead of being pulled-up by excess demand are also pushed-up as a result of a rise in the cost of production. Under cost-push inflation prices rise on account of a rise in the cost of raw materials, especially wages. The theory holds that the basic explanation for inflation is the fact that some producers, group of workers or both, succeed in raising the prices for either their product or services above the levels that would prevail under more competitive conditions.

In other words, inflationary pressures originate with supply rather than demand and spread throughout the economy. Inflation of the cost-push type originates in industries which are relatively concentrated and in which sellers can exercise considerable discretion in the formulation of both prices and wages. Cost-push inflation may not be possible in an economy characterized by pure competition.

Figure 32.7 shows that according to pure supply (cost-push) inflation theorists—in societies of oligopolies, unions and other pressure groups the aggregate supply curve moves upwards from S_0 to .$S_1$to S_2 whatever may happen to aggregate demand. A usual characteristic of such markets is that the money wage rate is inflexible downward, the result of which is an aggregate supply curve of the kind shown by S_0S. With the initial S_oS and D_0 curves in Figure 32.7, we can turn to the process by which increases in the money wage rate push up the price level. We assume that there is an increase in the money wage rate that results entirely from the exploitation of the market strength of labour unions and in no part from increased productivity of labour or increased demand for labour. An increase in wage rate has pushed S_0S curve to S_1S.

The price level at which each possible level of output will be supplied increases proportionally with the increase in the money wage rate. With aggregate demand of D_0, the result of the higher money wage rate and the resultant upward shift in SS function from S_0S to S_1S is a rise in the price level from P_0 to P_1 and a fall in the output level from Y_0 to Y_1 (which results in unemployment).

3. Mixed Demand Inflation: The problem of identifying the basic nature-and fundamental source of inflation continues. Does inflation arise from the demand side of the goods, factor and asset markets or from the supply side or from some combination of the two—the so-called mixed inflation. Many economists have come to believe that the actual process of inflation is neither due to demand-pull alone, nor due to cost-push alone, but due to a combination of both the elements of demand-pull and cost-push—called mixed inflation.

The process may be initiated either by demand-pull or by cost-push but it cannot be maintained unless other forces also operate activity. The major difference between the two theories of the inflationary process centres on the responsiveness of both the money wages and prices to changes in demand. Those who believe that there is wage and price flexibility in the economy argue in favour of demand-pull inflation; because such flexibility renders it impossible for any cost induced inflationary trend to sustain itself.

On the other hand, those who believe that wages and prices are not flexible emphasize the cost-push theory or inflation. Neither approach taken by itself should be considered a completely satisfactory explanation of the cause and nature of inflation—both the approaches are supplementary rather than competitive (or alternative) as explanations of the cause of inflation. The adjacent Figures showcases of mixed inflation.

One variety of mixed-inflation theory (in Fig. 32.9) denies for several reasons (one of the money illusion), that aggregate supply is price-inelastic at full employment. In Fig. 32.9 (Y_0, P_0), (Y_1, Y_1,) and (Y_2, P_2) are all full-employment positions in which no involuntary unemployment exists. The first corresponds to A.P. Lerner's "low full employment" with substantial voluntary unemployment, and the last to his "high full employment" with little or none.

The region between low and high full employment was called by Keynes "semi-inflation" in contrast to the true or full inflation. Mixed inflation theorists usually think society prefers the couple (Y_2, P_2) to other alternatives, even when all three are full-employment positions. In this type mixed inflation does not continue after (Y_2, P_2) is reached. In this respect, the solutions are related more closely to demand than to cost inflation.

Control Measures of Inflation:

A contractionary monetary policy is one common method of managing inflation. A contractionary policy aims to reduce the supply of money within an economy by lowering the prices of bonds and rising interest rates. Thus, consumption falls, prices fall and inflation slows down. Inflation can be controlled by a contractionary monetary policy is one common method of managing inflation. The aim of a contractionary policy is to reduce the supply of money within an economy by lowering the prices of bonds and rising interest rates. Thus, consumption falls, prices fall and inflation slows down.

Methods to Control Inflation:

The Central Bank and/or the government normally monitor inflation. Monetary policy is the key policy employed (changing interest rates). There are however several instruments to manage inflation in theory, including:

Monetary Policy: Higher interest rates decrease the economy's demand, resulting in lower economic growth and lower inflation.

Money supply management Monetarians claim that there is a near correlation between money supply and inflation, so inflation can be regulated by regulating the money supply.

Supply-side policies are policies designed to boost the economy's productivity and efficiency, placing downward pressure on long-term costs.

Fiscal Policy: A higher rate of income tax could reduce spending, demand, and inflationary pressures through fiscal policy.

Price limits may in principle, help alleviate inflationary pressures by attempting to regulate wages. Nonetheless, apart from the 1970s, it was scarcely used.

Measures to Check Inflation:

Inflation is an economic phenomenon that is used year after year to characterize rising prices for goods and services. This caused the consumer's buying power to decline because the rate of wage and income growth does not keep up with the rate of inflation.

Inflation management is not an easy mission, however. The rise in prices is due to several factors, such as aggregate demand, increased cash supply, etc. We need a lot of steps working in tandem to contain inflation.

Fiscal Measure to Control Inflation:

Government spending, public borrowing, and taxes comprise the Fiscal Policies to Combat Inflation. The Keynesian economists often referred to as "Fiscal," argue that due to an excess of aggregate demand over aggregate supply, demand-pull inflation is induced. Owing to spending by individuals, companies, and the government, aggregate demand rises (usually excessive spending by the government). This rise in demand due to the government or household spending can be effectively regulated by fiscal policies. Fiscal policy and fiscal initiatives are thus effective weapons of demand-pull inflation management. If the key trigger behind demand-pull inflation is government spending, then it can be regulated by reducing public expenditure. The public demand for goods and services declines with a decline in public spending, along with a decrease in private income and consumption expenditure. In cases where demand increases due to an increase in private spending, the most effective way to manage inflation is by taxing profits. The taxation of private income decreases the disposable income in question, and also reduces consumer spending. This has the effect of reducing aggregate demand.

In the event of a very high persistent inflation rate, both such steps may be taken simultaneously by the government to contain inflation. In the case of a decrease in public spending, the rate of taxes on private income is increased to keep demand under control. This form of policy of concurrently using both measures is called the "Surplus Budgeting Policy," which notes that "government should spend less than tax revenue".

- **Monetary Measures to Control Inflation:-**

Monetary interventions are aimed at reducing revenue from money.A moderate rate of inflation is considered desirable for the economy, and it varies from country to country and from time to time. As inflation crosses the desirable rate, several measures to control inflation are undertaken. Often, the countries use monetary measures to keep the situation under control.

(a) Management of Credit:

Monetary policy is one of the essential monetary interventions. A variety of strategies are employed by the country's central bank to regulate the quantity and quality of credit. To that end, bank rates are raised, securities are sold on the open market, the reserve ratio is raised and a range of selective credit management steps are taken, such as raising margin thresholds and controlling consumer credit. When inflation is due to cost-push variables, monetary policy will not be effective in managing inflation. Due to demand-pull variables, monetary policy can only be effective in managing inflation.

(b) Currency Demonetisation:

One of the monetary steps is to demonetize higher-denomination currencies. Such a step is typically taken when the country has a surplus of black currency.

(c) New Currency Issuance:

The problem of a new currency in place of the old currency is the most drastic monetary measure. Under this process, one new note is exchanged for several old currency notes. Likewise, the value of bank deposits is set accordingly. Such a measure is introduced when the issue of notes is excessive and hyperinflation occurs in the region. It is a measure that is very successful. But it is wrong because it affects the tiny depositors the most.

- **Fiscal Measures:**

Monetary policy alone is incapable of controlling inflation. It should, therefore, be supplemented by fiscal measures. Fiscal measures are highly effective for controlling government expenditure, personal consumption expenditure, and private and public investment.

The principal fiscal measures are the following:

(a) Reduction in Unnecessary Expenditure:

The government should reduce unnecessary expenditure on non-development activities in order to curb inflation. This will also put a check on private expenditure which is dependent upon government demand for goods and services. But it is not easy to cut government expenditure. Though this measure is always welcome but it becomes difficult to distinguish between essential and non-essential expenditure. Therefore, this measure should be supplemented by taxation.

(b) Increase in Taxes:

To cut personal consumption expenditure, the rates of personal, corporate and commodity taxes should be raised and even new taxes should be levied, but the rates of taxes should not be so high as to discourage saving, investment and production. Rather, the tax system should provide larger incentives to those who save, invest and produce more.

Further, to bring more revenue into the tax-net, the government should penalise the tax evaders by imposing heavy fines. Such measures are bound to be effective in controlling inflation. To increase the supply of goods within the country, the government should reduce import duties and increase export duties.

(c) Increase in Savings:

Another measure is to increase savings on the part of the people. This will tend to reduce disposable income with the people, and hence personal consumption expenditure. But due to the rising cost of living, people are not in a position to save much voluntarily.

Keynes, therefore, advocated compulsory savings or what he called 'deferred payment' where the saver gets his money back after some years. For this purpose, the government should float public loans carrying high rates of interest, start saving schemes with prize money, or lottery for long periods, etc. It should also introduce compulsory provident fund, provident fund-cum-pension schemes, etc. All such measures increase savings and are likely to be effective in controlling inflation.

(d) Surplus Budgets:

An important measure is to adopt anti-inflationary budgetary policy. For this purpose, the government should give up deficit financing and instead have surplus budgets. It means collecting more in revenues and spending less.

(e) Public Debt:

At the same time, it should stop repayment of public debt and postpone it to some future date till inflationary pressures are controlled within the economy. Instead, the government should borrow more to reduce money supply with the public.

Like monetary measures, fiscal measures alone cannot help in controlling inflation. They should be supplemented by monetary, non-monetary and non-fiscal measures.

3. Other Measures:

The other types of measures are those which aim at increasing aggregate supply and reducing aggregate demand directly.

(a) To Increase Production:

The following measures should be adopted to increase production:

(i) One of the foremost measures to control inflation is to increase the production of essential consumer goods like food, clothing, kerosene oil, sugar, vegetable oils, etc.

(ii) If there is need, raw materials for such products may be imported on preferential basis to increase the production of essential commodities,

(iii) Efforts should also be made to increase productivity. For this purpose, industrial peace should be maintained through agreements with trade unions, binding them not to resort to strikes for some time,

(iv) The policy of rationalisation of industries should be adopted as a long-term measure. Rationalisation increases productivity and production of industries through the use of brain, brawn and bullion,

(v) All possible help in the form of latest technology, raw materials, financial help, subsidies, etc. should be provided to different consumer goods sectors to increase production.

(b) Rational Wage Policy:

Another important measure is to adopt a rational wage and income policy. Under hyperinflation, there is a wage-price spiral. To control this, the government should freeze wages, incomes, profits, dividends, bonus, etc.

But such a drastic measure can only be adopted for a short period as it is likely to antagonise both workers and industrialists. Therefore, the best course is to link increase in wages to increase in productivity. This will have a dual effect. It will control wages and at the same time increase productivity, and hence raise production of goods in the economy.

(c) Price Control:

Price control and rationing is another measure of direct control to check inflation. Price control means fixing an upper limit for the prices of essential consumer goods. They are the maximum prices fixed by law and anybody charging more than these prices is punished by law. But it is difficult to administer price control.

(d) Rationing:

Rationing aims at distributing consumption of scarce goods so as to make them available to a large number of consumers. It is applied to essential consumer goods such as wheat, rice, sugar, kerosene oil, etc. It is meant to stabilise the prices of necessaries and assure distributive justice. But it is very inconvenient for consumers because it leads to queues, artificial shortages, corruption and black marketing. Keynes did not favour rationing for it "involves a great deal of waste, both of resources and of employment."

Thus, these are the major monetary measures that countries use to keep the inflationary pressures under control or maintain the desirable limit of inflation.From the various monetary, fiscal and other measures discussed above, it becomes clear that to control inflation, the government should adopt all measures simultaneously. Inflation is like a hydra- headed monster which should be fought by using all the weapons at the command of the government.

CHAPTER III

International Trade and Foreign Policy

International Trade

International trade is the exchange of goods and services between countries.

Trading globally gives consumers and countries the opportunity to be exposed to goods and services not available in their own countries, or more expensive domestically.The importance of international trade was recognized early on by political economists such as Adam Smith and David Ricardo. Still, some argue that international trade can actually be bad for smaller nations, putting them at a greater disadvantage on the world stage.

Understanding International Trade

International trade was key to the rise of the global economy. In the global economy, supply and demand—and thus prices—both impact and are impacted by global events.

Political change in Asia, for example, could result in an increase in the cost of labor. This could increase the manufacturing costs for an American sneaker company that is based in Malaysia, which would then result in an increase in the price charged for a pair of sneakers that an American consumer might purchase at their local mall.

Imports and Exports

A product that is sold to the global market is called an export, and a product that is bought from the global market is an import. Imports and exports are accounted for in the current account section of a country's balance of payments.

Global trade allows wealthy countries to use their resources—for example, labor, technology, or capital—more efficiently. Different countries are endowed with different assets and natural resources: land, labor, capital, technology, etc.

This allows some countries to produce the same good more efficiently; in other words, more quickly and at a lower cost. Therefore, they may sell it more cheaply than other countries. If a country cannot efficiently produce an item, it can obtain it by trading with another country that can. This is known as specialization in international trade.

For example, England and Portugal have historically both benefited by specializing and trading according to their comparative advantages. Portugal has plentiful vineyards and can make wine at a low cost, while England is able to more cheaply manufacture cloth given its pastures are full of sheep.

Each country would eventually recognize these facts and stop attempting to make the product that was more costly to generate domestically in favor of engaging in trade. Indeed, over time, England stopped producing wine, and Portugal stopped manufacturing cloth. Both countries saw that it was to their advantage to stop their efforts at producing these items at home and, instead, to trade with each other in order to acquire them.

India's Foreign Trade Policy

The Department of Commerce has the mandate to make India a major player in global trade and assume a role of leadership in international trade organizations commensurate with India's growing importance. The Department devises commodity and country-specific strategy in the medium term and strategic plan/vision and India's Foreign Trade Policy in the long run.

India's Foreign Trade Policy (FTP) provides the basic framework of policy and strategy for promoting exports and trade. It is periodically reviewed to adapt to the changing domestic and international scenario.

The Department is also responsible for multilateral and bilateral commercial relations, special economic zones (SEZs), state trading, export promotion and trade facilitation, and development and regulation of certain export oriented industries and commodities.

The current Foreign Trade Policy (2015-20) focusses on improving India's market share in existing markets and products as well as exploring new products and new markets. India's Foreign Trade Policy also envisages helping exporters leverage benefits of GST, closely monitoring export performances, improving ease of trading across borders, increasing realization from India's agriculture-based exports and promoting exports from MSMEs and labour intensive sectors. The DoC has also sought to make states active partners in exports. As a consequence, state governments are now actively developing export strategies based on the strengths of their respective sectors.

While the external environment has a major role to play in the success of export policies, it is also critical to address constraints within India including infrastructure bottlenecks, high transaction costs, complex procedures, constraints in manufacturing and inadequate diversification in India's services exports. India is a signatory to the Trade Facilitation Agreement (TFA) at the WTO, which will contribute to the simplification and lowering of transaction costs.

According to current WTO rules as well as those under negotiation India needs to eventually phase out subsidies and move towards fundamental systemic measures in the future. Under the Agreement on Subsidies, India has moved on from Annex VII countries of WTO on breaching the US$ 1,000 per capita income benchmark for 3 consecutive years in 2015.

The present Commerce & Industry Minister Shri Piyush Goyal has also asserted that India needs to evolve from a dependence on subsidies, "I do not think that any programme or ambitious scheme can run only on subsidies and government help. We have to move out of this continuous effort and demand and make our industry truly competitive and self-reliant."

The government is looking to focus on promoting exports of high value-added products, where India has a strong domestic manufacturing base, including engineering goods, electronics, drugs and pharmaceuticals, textiles and agriculture. This is apart from the continued push to AYUSH and the Indian services sector.

Around 70% of India's exports constitute products that have just 30% share in global trade. The government is looking at some more promising product groups like defence equipment, medical devices, agro-processing, technical textiles and chemicals.

In 2018, then Commerce & Industry Minister Shri Suresh Prabhu envisaged a strategy to double India's exports by 2025. The approach included devising a commodity-specific strategy for key sectors like gems and jewellery, leather, textile & apparel, engineering sector, electronics, chemicals and petrochemicals, pharma, agri and allied products and marine products. Territory specific strategy will cover North American Free Trade Agreement (NAFTA), Europe, North East Asia, ASEAN, South Asia, Latin America, Africa and WANA, Australia, New Zealand, and CIS.

The theory of international trade

Comparative-advantage analysis

The British school of classical economics began in no small measure as a reaction against the inconsistencies of mercantilist thought. Adam Smith was the 18th-century founder of this school; as mentioned above, his famous work, The Wealth of Nations (1776), is in part an antimercantilist tract. In the book, Smith emphasized the importance of specialization as a source of increased output, and he treated international trade as a particular instance of specialization: in a world where productive resources are scarce and human wants cannot be completely satisfied, each nation should specialize in the production of goods it is particularly well equipped to produce; it should export part of this production, taking in exchange other goods that it cannot so readily turn out. Smith did not expand these ideas at much length, but another classical economist, David Ricardo, developed them into the principle of comparative advantage, a principle still to be found, much as Ricardo spelled it out, in contemporary textbooks on international trade.

Comparative Advantage

These two countries realized that they could produce more by focusing on those products for which they have a comparative advantage. In such a case, the Portuguese would begin to produce only wine, and the English only cotton. Each country can now create a specialized output of 20 units per year and trade equal proportions of both products. As such, each country now has access to both products at lower costs. We can see then that for both countries, the opportunity cost of producing both products is greater than the cost of specializing.

Comparative advantage can contrast with absolute advantage. Absolute advantage leads to unambiguous gains from specialization and trade only in cases wherein each producer has an absolute advantage in producing some good. If a producer lacked any absolute advantage, then they would never export anything. But we do see that countries without any clear absolute advantage do gain from trade because they have a comparative advantage.

Origins of Comparative Advantage

The theory of comparative advantage has been attributed to the English political economist David Ricardo. Comparative advantage is discussed in Ricardo's book On the Principles of Political Economy and Taxation, published in 1817, although it has been suggested that Ricardo's mentor, James Mill, likely originated the analysis and slipped it into Ricardo's book on the sly.123

Comparative advantage, as we have shown above, famously showed how England and Portugal both benefit by specializing and trading according to their comparative advantages. In this case, Portugal was able to make wine at a low cost, while England was able to cheaply manufacture cloth. Ricardo predicted that each country would eventually recognize these facts and stop attempting to make the product that was more costly to generate.

IMPORTANT:- According to the international trade theory, even if a country has an absolute advantage over another, it can still benefit from specialization.

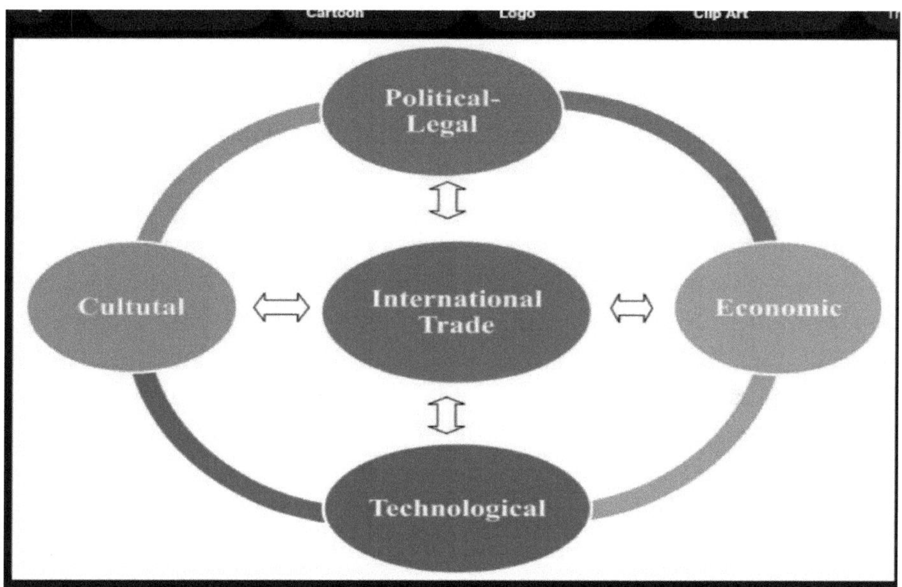

simplynotes.in

Criticisms of Comparative Advantage

Why doesn't the world have open trading between countries? When there is free trade, why do some countries remain poor at the expense of others? There are many reasons, but the most influential is something that economists call rent seeking. Rent seeking occurs when one group organizes and lobbies the government to protect its interests.

Say, for example, the producers of American shoes understand and agree with the free-trade argument but also know that cheaper foreign shoes would negatively impact their narrow interests. Even if laborers would be most productive by switching from making shoes to making computers, nobody in the shoe industry wants to lose their job or see profits decrease in the short run.

Sources of comparative advantage

As already noted, British classical economists simply accepted the fact that productivity differences exist between countries; they made no concerted attempt to explain which commodities a country would export or import. During the 20th century, international economists offered a number of theories in an effort to explain why countries have differences in productivity, the factor that determines comparative advantage and the pattern of international trade.

Natural resources

First, countries can have an advantage because they are richly endowed with a particular natural resource. For example, countries with plentiful oil resources can generally produce oil inexpensively. Because Saudi Arabia produces oil very cheaply, it holds a comparative advantage in oil, and it exports oil in order to finance its purchases of imports. Similarly, countries with large forests generally are the major exporters of wood, paper, and paper products. The supply available for export also depends on domestic demand. Canada has large quantities of lumber available for export to the United States, not only because of its large areas of forest but also because its small population consumes little of the supply, leaving much of the lumber available for export. Climate is another natural resource that provides an export advantage. Thus, for example, bananas are exported by Central American countries—not Iceland or Finland.

Amplification of the theory

At a later stage in the history of comparative-advantage theory, English philosopher and political economist John Stuart Mill showed that the determination of the exact after-trade price ratio was a supply-and-demand problem. At each possible intermediate ratio (within the range of 1:2 and 1:3), country A would want to import a particular quantity of wine and export a particular quantity of cloth. At that same possible ratio, country B would also wish to import and export particular amounts of cloth and of wine. For any intermediate ratio taken at random, however, A's export-import quantities are unlikely to match those of B. Ordinarily, there will be just one intermediate ratio at which the quantities correspond; that is the final trading ratio at which quantities exchanged will stabilize. Indeed, once they have stabilized, there is no further profit in exchanging goods. Even with such profits eliminated, however, there is no reason why A producers should want to stop selling part of their cloth in B, since the return there is as good as that obtained from domestic sales. Furthermore, any falloff in the amounts exported and imported would reintroduce profit opportunities.

In this simple example, based on labour costs, the result is complete (and unrealistic) specialization: country A's entire labour force will move to cloth production and country B's to wine production. More elaborate comparative-advantage models recognize production costs other than labour (that is, the costs of land and of capital). In such models, part of country A's wine industry may survive and compete effectively against imports, as may also part of B's cloth industry. The models can be expanded in other ways—for example, by involving more than two countries or products, by adding transport costs, or by accommodating a number of other variables such as labour conditions and product quality. The essential conclusions, however, come from the elementary model used above, so that this model, despite its simplicity, still provides a workable outline of the theory. (It should be noted that even the most elaborate comparative-advantage models continue to rely on certain simplifying assumptions without which the basic conclusions do not necessarily hold. These assumptions are discussed below.)

As noted earlier, the effect of this analysis is to correct any false first impression that low-productivity countries are at a hopeless disadvantage in trading with high-productivity ones. The impression is false, that is, if one assumes, as comparative-advantage theory does, that international trade is an exchange of goods between countries. It is pointless for country A to sell goods to country B, whatever its labour-cost advantages, if there is nothing that it can profitably take back in exchange for its sales. With one exception, there will always be at least one commodity that a low-productivity country such as B can successfully export. Country B must of course pay a price for its low productivity, as compared with A; but that price is a lower per capita domestic income and not a disadvantage in international trading. For trading purposes, absolute productivity levels are unimportant; country B will always find one or more commodities in which it enjoys a comparative advantage (that is, a commodity in the production of which its absolute disadvantage is least). The one exception is that case in which productivity ratios, and consequently pretrade price ratios, happen to match one another in two countries. This would have been the case had country B required four labour hours (instead of six) to produce a unit of cloth. In such a circumstance, there would be no incentive for either country to engage in trade, nor would there be any gain from trading. In a two-commodity example such as that employed, it might not be unusual to find matching productivity and price ratios. But as soon as one moves on to cases of three and more commodities, the statistical probability of encountering precisely equal ratios becomes very small indeed.

Trade in services

India was the eighth largest exporter of commercial services in the world in 2016, accounting for 3.4% of global trade in services. India recorded a 5.7% growth in services trade in 2016–17

Exports and imports

India exports approximately 7500 commodities to about 190 countries, and imports around 6000 commodities from 140 countries.[11] India exported US$318.2 billion and imported $462.9 billion worth of commodities in 2014.

The Government of India's Economic Survey 2017–18 noted that five states — Maharashtra, Gujarat, Karnataka, Tamil Nadu and Telangana — accounted for 70% of India's total exports. It was the first time that the survey included international export data for states. The survey found a high correlation between a state's Gross State Domestic Product (GSDP) per capita and its share of total exports. With a high GSDP per capita but low export share, Kerala was the only major outlier because remittances heavily influenced the state's GSDP per capita.

The survey also found that the largest firms in India contributed to a smaller percentage of exports when compared to countries like Brazil, Germany, Mexico, and the United States. The top 1% of India's companies accounted for 38% of total exports.

The provisional data for March exports, released by the Ministry of Commerce at the end of April, reveals a grim situation. As per the data, India's exports during March 2020 accounted for a little over $21.4 billion, despite a promising performance in just the previous month. This fall of approximately 35% year-on-year, as compared to March 2019 ($32.72 billion), is touching a multi-year low, and the figures are bound to fall further. A key thing to note is that exports have fallen across almost all of the commodity groups. Some commodities have registered a decline by over 30-40%, particularly engineering goods, textiles, meat, cereals, plastics and chemicals, which have been the major growth drivers of exports in recent years. As an immediate aftermath of the spread of the COVID-19 pandemic to multiple countries, global demand has fallen significantly and many orders have been cancelled. Further, the disruption of supply chains due to the ongoing lockdown has aggravated the poor performance of Indian exports -- and the situation is likely to worsen in the coming months, before recovery starts. India's electrical machinery and equipment has 40 per cent dependence on imports from China. However this number has reduced from 59.5 per cent in FY18 to 40 per cent in FY19. Although India has increased production of low-end electronic components. Import dependency on China is its major limitation. The automobile sector, which accounts for 7.5 per cent of India's GDP and a massive 49 per cent of the manufacturing GDP, is already facing slowdown. The coronavirus lockdown has made the situation worse for the auto sector as 10 to 30 per cent of automotive components are supplied from China. If factories do not resume activity in China, it could adversely affect the sector.

Trading partners of India

US has indeed arisen as the biggest exchanging accomplice of India with respective product exchange of USD 67.41 billion. The US has been the biggest exchanging accomplice of India as for stock exchange beginning around 2018-19, besides in 2020-21, when exchange with America declined possibly because of the COVID-19 pandemic, Minister of State for Commerce and Industry Anupriya Patel said in a composed answer to the Rajya Sabha.

"In the ongoing 2021-22 (April-October), the US has indeed turned into the biggest exchanging accomplice with two-sided stock exchange of USD 67.41 billion, representing 11.98 percent of India's all out stock exchange," she said.

She likewise said that India's respective exchange with Australia has expanded to USD 13.88 billion of every 2021, from USD 7.48 billion in the relating time of 2020.

Essentially, the respective exchange with UAE has developed to USD 49.06 billion of every 2021, from USD 29.48 billion out of 2020 for a similar period." The reciprocal exchange with Belgium has additionally developed to USD 13.70 in 2021, from USD 7.63 billion out of 2020 for a similar period," she added.

In a different answer, Patel said the portion of product of labor and products in GDP has expanded to 18.7 percent during 2020-21, over 18.4 percent in 2019-20, and 21.7 percent in 2021-22 (April-September) over 19.4 percent in 2020-21 (April-September).

In another answer, she said India's import of heartbeats plunged hardly to 10,34,491 ton in a similar period last year. It was 24,66,156 ton in 2020-21 as against 28,98,078 ton in 2019-20.

In an inquiry whether it's undeniably true that the service has arranged an arrangement to assemble a 5-star inn at Pragati Maidan, Patel said: "OK". The development has not begun at this point, she said.

Further information: List of the largest trading partners of India

India's largest trading partners in order of value of total trade are Bangladesh, Bhutan, Germany, Hong Kong, Iraq, Israel, Japan, Nepal, Russia, Saudi Arabia, China, Singapore, Switzerland, the United Arab Emirates and the United States. India is biggest exporter of pharmaceuticals, some food products and is a mixed economy.

Largest trading partners with India [edit]

India's largest trade partners with their total trade (sum of imports and exports) in billions of US dollars for the financial year 2019–20 were as follows:

Rank	Country	Exports	Imports	Total Trade	Trade Balance
1	United States	73.3	40.3	113.6	33.0
2	China	16.61	65.26	81.87	-48.65
3	United Arab Emirates	28.81	30.22	59.03	-1.41
4	Saudi Arabia	6.39	20.32	26.71	-13.93
5	Switzerland	1.21	16.9	18.11	-15.69
6	Germany	8.21	13.69	21.9	-5.48
7	Hong Kong	13.7	20.34	34.04	-6.64
8	Indonesia	4.12	15.06	19.18	-10.94
9	South Korea	4.85	15.65	20.5	-10.8
10	Malaysia	3.71	9.08	16.93	-5.30
11	Singapore	7.72	9.31	16.93	-1.59
12	Nigeria	2.22	9.95	16.36	-11.00
13	Belgium	5.03	8.26	16.33	-5.29
14	Qatar	0.90	9.02	15.66	-13.56
15	Japan	4.66	9.85	15.52	-4.75
16	Iraq	1.00	10.84	15.08	-13.42
17	Kuwait	1.25	4.97	14.58	-12.18
18	United Kingdom	8.83	5.19	14.34	4.30
19	Iran	2.78	6.28	13.13	-4.78
20	Australia	3.26	8.90	13.03	-7.47
21	Venezuela	0.13	5.70	11.99	-11.47
22	South Africa	3.59	5.95	11.72	-3.40
-	*Remaining Countries*	126.78	104.92	231.70	21.86
India's Total		**330.08**	**514.08**	**844.16**	**-184.0**

wikipedia.org

Export partners [edit]

India exports approximately 7500 commodities to about 192 countries.[7] The following table shows India's 10 largest destinations for exports in 2019–2020.[8]

Rank	Country	Value (US$ billion)	Share of overall exports
1	United States	57.7	16.94%
2	United Arab Emirates	28.8	9.20%
3	China	16.6	5.47%
4	Hong Kong	10.9	3.63%
5	Singapore	8.9	2.90%
6	United Kingdom	8.7	2.80%
7	Netherlands	8.3	2.69%
8	Germany	8.29	2.65%
9	Bangladesh	8.20	2.61%
10	Nepal	7.16	2.28%

Import partners [edit]

India imports around 6000 commodities from 140 countries.[7] The following table shows India's 10 largest sources of imports in 2019–2020.[8]

Rank	Country	Value (US$ billion)	Share of overall imports
1	China	57.8	14.37%
2	United States	30.5	7.57%
3	United Arab Emirates	25.8	6.39%
4	Saudi Arabia	23.0	5.70%
5	Iraq	19.8	4.91%
6	Switzerland	14.8	3.67%
7	Hong Kong	14.6	3.63%
8	South Korea	13.2	3.28%
9	Indonesia	12.8	3.17%
10	Singapore	12.2	3.02%

wikipedia.org

Benefits or Some advantages of International Trade:

- **Optimal utilization of regular assets:**

Worldwide exchange assists every country with utilizing its normal assets. Every nation can focus on creation of those products for which its assets are the most appropriate. Wastage of assets is stayed away from.

- **Availability of a wide range of goods:**

It empowers a country to get products which it can't create or which it isn't delivering because of greater expenses, by bringing in from different nations at lower costs.

- **Specialization:**

Unfamiliar exchange prompts specialization and energizes creation of various products in various nations. Products can be created for a relatively minimal price because of benefits of division of work.

- **Advantages of enormous scope production:**

Due to global exchange, merchandise are created for home utilization as well as for commodity to different nations moreover. Countries of the world can discard products which they have in surplus in the worldwide business sectors. This prompts creation overall scale and the benefits of huge scope creation can be gotten by every one of the nations of the world.

- **Stability in costs:**

Worldwide exchange figures out wild vacillations costs. It balances the costs of merchandise all through the world (overlooking expense of transportation, and so forth.)

- **Exchange of specialized expertise and foundation of new industries:**

Underdeveloped nations can lay out and foster new ventures with the apparatus, gear and specialized ability imported from created nations. This aids in the improvement of these nations and the economy of the world overall.

- **Increase in productivity:**

Because of worldwide rivalry, the makers in a national endeavour to create better quality merchandise and at the base conceivable expense. This builds proficiency and advantages to the buyers everywhere.

- **Development of the method for transport and communication:**

International exchange requires the best method for transport and correspondence. For the upsides of global exchange, advancement in the method for transport and correspondence is likewise made conceivable.

- **International co-activity and understanding:**

Individuals of various nations interact with one another. Business intercourse among countries of the world supports trade of thoughts and culture. It makes co-activity, grasping, genial relations among different countries.

- **Ability to confront normal calamities:**

Natural catastrophes, for example, dry season, floods, starvation, tremor and so on, influence the creation of a nation antagonistically. Lack in the stockpile of products at the hour of such regular catastrophes can be met by imports from different nations.

- **Other benefits:**

Worldwide exchange helps numerous alternate ways like advantages to shoppers, global harmony and better way of life.

Limitations of International trade

The global economy has made it easier to ship products or sell a service almost anywhere in the world. Overnight shipping, e-commerce, language translators and established international marketplaces have made this accessible to businesses of all sizes. However, there are several disadvantages of international trade that you may need to be overcome if your company is to be truly successful in these marketplaces.

Here are a few of the Limitations or disadvantages of international trade:

Foreign trade does not always amount to blessings.

- **Rapid Depletion of Exhaustible Natural Resources:**

It could lead to a more rapid depletion of exhaustible natural resources.

As countries begin to up their production levels, natural resources tend to get depleted with the time and it could pose a dangerous threat to the future generation.

- **Import of Harmful Goods:**

Foreign trade may lead to the import of harmful goods like cigarettes, drugs, etc., which may harm the health of the residents of the country. For example, the people of China suffered greatly through opium imports.

- **Disadvantages of International Shipping Customs and Duties**

International shipping companies make it easy to ship packages almost anywhere in the world.

However, one of the disadvantages of international trade is that most of these destination countries' customs agencies charge extra fees on items shipped to them.

While each government determines the duties and taxes differently, it is typically calculated on the value of the products sent (item, insurance plus shipping). The item description may also affect these fees based on what it is made of or used for.

In addition to the cost of their product, a company needs to understand what the end consumer will be charged by the international shipping company. This is sometimes referred to as the "landed cost."

- **It may Exhaust Resources:**

International trade leads to intensive cultivation of land. Thus, it has the operations of law of diminishing returns in agricultural countries. It also makes a nation poor by giving too much burden over the resources.

- **Over Specialization:**

Overspecialization may be disastrous for a country. A substitute may appear and ruin the economic lives of millions.

- **The danger of Starvation:**

A country might depend for its food mainly on foreign countries. In times of war, there is a serious danger of starvation for such countries.

- **Servicing Customers**

After international customers make a purchase, how will they be serviced when they are so far away? Again, language and cultural differences need to be considered to overcome one of the major disadvantages of international trade.

Your company needs to be prepared up front to communicate with these customers in different time zones, preferably in their language. If you're not able to staff 24/7, expectations for when a reply will be received need to be set up front.

- **One Country Gains at the Expense of Other:**

One of the serious drawbacks of foreign trade is that one country may gain at the expense of other due to certain accidental advantages. For example, the Industrial Revolution is Great Britain ruined Indian handicrafts during the nineteenth century.

- **May Lead to War:**

Foreign trade may lead to war different countries compete with each other in finding out new markets and sources of raw material for their industries and frequently come into the clash. This was one of the causes of first and Second World War.

- **Language Diversity:**

Each country has its own language. As foreign trade involves trade between two or more countries, there is the diversity of languages. This difference in language creates problem in foreign trade.

- **Intellectual Property Theft**

The wider a product is distributed, the more likely that it may be illegally copied by a competitor. This can be in the form of proprietary information or market branding.

With cross-country borders, it becomes very difficult for a company to prosecute. However, copyrighting in the U.S. can help protect a company as long as the country where the product is sold has signed an international intellectual protection treaty. Some countries also have their own separate copyright and trademark protections that can be filed to protect companies selling products in their countries.

Finally, there is always a political risk of international trade. Governments and their policies change over time, and sometimes companies can get stuck in the middle with different regulations that may target their sales and customers. This is why it may be good to market products to a geographic region, rather than a single country, to help balance the company's risk.

CHAPTER IV

Balance of Trade and Balance of Payments

Balance of Trade

Balance of Trade is the differentiation between the worth of a country's imports and products for a given time frame outline. The BoT is the biggest constituent of a country's equilibrium of installments. Financial specialists use the BoT to figure the cooperative power of a country's economy. The BoT is otherwise called the exchange balance or the global exchange.

The balance of trade is the value of a country's exports minus its imports. It's the biggest component of the balance of payments that measures all international transactions. It's easy to measure since all goods and many services pass through the customs office.

The balance of trade excess is generally great for homegrown makers liable for the commodities. Be that as it may, this is likewise prone to be ominous to homegrown buyers of the products who follow through on greater expenses.

On the other hand, The balance of trade of import/export imbalance is generally troublesome to homegrown makers in contest with the imports, however it can likewise be ideal for homegrown buyers of the products who follow through on lower costs.

The trade balance is also the biggest part of the current account. It measures a country's net income earned on international assets. It's the trade balance plus any other payments across borders.

Key Takeaways

- A positive trade balance (surplus) is when exports exceed imports.
- A negative trade balance (deficit) is when exports are less than imports.
- Use the balance of trade to compare a country's economy to its trading partners.
- A trade surplus is harmful only when the government uses protectionism.
- A trade deficit can be beneficial to countries that import heavily and simultaneously invest in economic development.

How to Calculate It

A country's trade balance equals the value of its exports minus its imports.

The formula is X - M = TB, where:

X = Exports

M = Imports

TB = Trade Balance

Exports are goods or services made domestically and sold to a foreigner. That includes a pair of jeans you mail to a friend overseas. It could also be signage a corporate headquarter transfers to its foreign office. If the foreigner pays for it, then it's an export.

Imports are goods and services bought by a country's residents but made in a foreign country. It includes souvenirs purchased by tourists traveling abroad. Services provided while traveling, such as transportation, hotels, and meals, are also imports. It doesn't matter whether the company that makes the good or service is a domestic or foreign company. If it was purchased or made in a foreign country, it's an import.

When a country's exports are greater than its imports, it has a trade surplus. When exports are less than imports, it has a trade deficit. On the surface, a surplus is preferable to a deficit. However, this is an overly simplistic assumption. A trade deficit is not inherently bad, as it can be indicative of a strong economy. Moreover, when coupled with prudent investment decisions, a deficit can lead to stronger economic growth in the future.

Balance of Payments

Balance of Payments is an assertion of the relative multitude of exchanges that are made between elements in a single country and the remainder of the world over a specific time period, like a quarter or a year. To place it at the end of the day, the BoP is a bunch of records that recognizes every one of the business exchanges worked by the country in a particular period with the leftover countries of the world. It reports a record of the multitude of financial exchanges performed universally by the country on merchandise, administrations, and pay during the year.

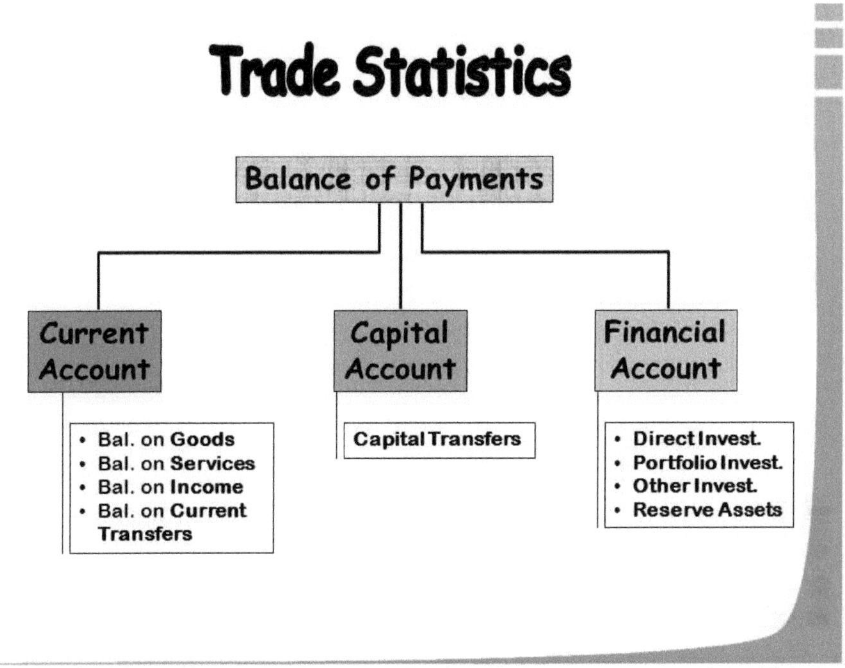

slideplayer.com

Understanding the Balance of Payments (BOP)

The equilibrium of installments (BOP) exchanges comprise of imports and products of merchandise, administrations, and capital, as well as move installments, like unfamiliar guide and settlements. A nation's equilibrium between installments and its net worldwide venture position together establish its global records.

The equilibrium of installments isolates exchanges into two records: the ongoing record and the capital record. Now and again the capital record is known as the monetary record, with a different, typically tiny, capital record recorded independently. The ongoing record remembers exchanges for merchandise, administrations, speculation pay, and current exchanges.

The capital record, comprehensively characterized, remembers exchanges for monetary instruments and national bank holds. Barely characterized, it remembers just exchanges for monetary instruments. The ongoing record is remembered for estimations of public result, while the capital record isn't.

Assuming a nation trades a thing (an ongoing record exchange), it actually imports unfamiliar capital when that thing is paid for (a capital record exchange). In the event that a nation can't finance its imports through products of capital, it should do as such by running down its stores. The present circumstance is frequently alluded to as an equilibrium of installments shortage, utilizing the restricted meaning of the capital record that avoids national bank saves. In actuality, in any case, the extensively characterized equilibrium of installments should amount to zero by definition.

Practically speaking, measurable disparities emerge because of the trouble of precisely counting each exchange between an economy and the remainder of the world, including errors brought about by unfamiliar cash interpretations.

This chapter is a prepared reckoner guide for the understudies to become familiar with the contrast between the harmony between exchange and equilibrium of installments.

Basis	Balance of Trade (BOT)	Balance of Payments (BOP)
1. Nature of transactions	Transactions concerning trade of goods only are recorded.	All transactions concerning goods, services and capital transfers are recorded.
2. Capital transactions	Transactions of capital nature are not included in Balance of Trade.	Transactions of capital nature are also recorded in Balance of Payment.
3. Mutual relation	Balance of Trade is a part of current account of Balance of Payment.	BOP is much larger as it has current and capital accounts which include BOP too.
4. Favourable BOT/BOP	When exports of goods are higher than the imports of goods, BOT is considered as favourable.	When net balance of current account and capital account is in plus. BOP is considered as favourable.

qsstudy.com

Balance of Payment

It is a statement that contains the transactions made by residents of a particular country with the rest of the world over a specific time period. It is also known as the balance of international payments and is often abbreviated as BOP. It summarizes all payments and receipts by firms, individuals, and the government. The transactions can be both factor payments and transfer payments.

There are two accounts in the BOP statement: The **Current Account** and the **Capital Account**. The Current Account records all transactions involving goods, services, investment income, and current transfer payments. The Capital Account shows the net change in ownership of foreign assets and transactions in financial instruments.

The balance of payments account follows a double-entry system. All receipts are entered on the credit side, whereas all payments are entered on the debit side. Theoretically, a balance of payments accounts is always zero, with the total on the debit side equaling the total on the credit side. Practically, however, there might be an error of some degree due to the different sources of data and fluctuation of currency exchange rates.

2.2 Balance of payment on Capital Accounts

The capital account is used to finance the deficit in the current account or absorb the surplus in the current account. The three major components of capital account are:

1. **Loans to and Borrowings from abroad**

These consist of all loans and borrowings given to or received from abroad. It includes both private sector loans, as well as public sector loans.

1. **Investments to/from abroad**

These are investments made by non-residents in shares in the home country or investments in real estate in any other country.

3. **Changes in Foreign Exchange Reserves**

Foreign exchange reserves are maintained by the central bank to control the exchange rate and ultimately balance the BOP.

A Current account deficit is financed by a surplus in the Capital account and vice versa. This can be done by borrowing more money from abroad or lending more money to non-residents.

Balance of payment on Current Account

The four major components of the Current account are as follows:

1. **Visible trade**

This is the net of export and imports of goods (visible items). The balance of this visible trade is known as the trade balance. There is a trade deficit when imports are higher than exports and a trade surplus when exports are higher than imports.

2. **Invisible trade**

This is the net of export and imports of services (invisible items). Transactions mainly consists of shipping, IT, banking and insurance services.

3. **Unilateral transfers to and from abroad**

These refer to payments that are not factor payments – for example, gifts or donations sent to the resident of a country by a non-resident relative.

4. **Income receipts and payments**

These include factor payments and receipts. These are generally rent on property, interest on capital, and profits on investments.

Equilibrium and Disequilibrium in BOP

When the demand and supply of any foreign currency in a country in a given time period is equal, it is termed as 'Equilibrium position' in the balance of payment. While a disequilibrium means that the condition is either deficit or surplus.

The surplus in the balance of payment occurs when the total payments are exceeded by the total receipts. Similarly, a deficit occurs when the total receipts are exceeded by total payments.

CAUSES OF DISEQUILIBRIUM IN BALANCE OF PAYMENTS:

1. **Natural Causes:**

Natural Calamities like famines, droughts, earthquakes, floods etc. cause disequilibrium in

balance of payment, Imports of a country multiply under the impact of these calamities leading to disequilibrium in balance of payments.

Economics Development Plans:

Heavy dose of investment is main cause of disequilibrium in balance of payment. Developing countries have to depend on developed foreign countries for their economic development.

3. **Price Cost Effect:**

On account of development planning, costs and prices in export industries generally go

up. It leads to fall in the total volume of experts and balance of payments becomes adverse.

4. **Cyclical Fluctuations:**

Business cycles in international sphere also disequilibrium in balance of payments.

5. **Population Explosion:**

Due to rapid increase in population, aggregate consumption demand in under

developed countries increase. Consequently, export surplus falls down and balance of payments becomes adverse.

6. **Political factors:**

Political instability of the country may also have adverse affect on the balance of payments

of country. If the international relations of a country is full of tense, these may have unfavorable on the balance of payments

MEASURES TO CORRECT ADVERSE BALANCE OF PAYMENTS

If a balance of payments (bop) disequilibrium persists for an extended period of time, it has a negative impact on the economy. It is critical to eliminate disequilibrium, particularly a deficit. There are several ways to correct a balance of payments imbalance.

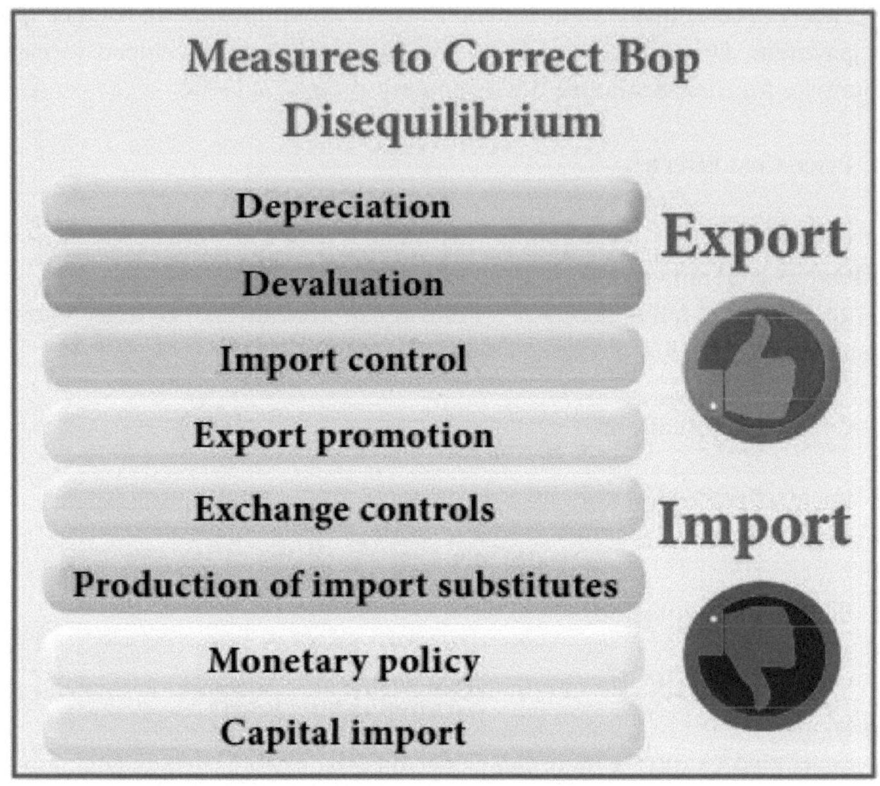

Brainkart.com

These measures are classified into two types: monetary measures and non-monetary measures

1. **Deflation**

Deflation refers to that monetary policy under which the volume of currency is reduced; consequently, prices and monetary income of the people are brought down. In India, Reserve Bank of India, the Central Bank contracts the volume of credit in the economy by using quantitative and qualitative methods of credit control (raising the Bank rate and open market operations)

2. **Devaluation**

Devaluation is that monetary measure under which government of a country lowers the value of its currency in terms of foreign currencies. Therefore, imports become dearer and exports cheaper. In this way adverse BOP is corrected

3. **Exchange depreciation**

If in the international sphere, rate of exchange is flexible, government need not resort to policy of devaluation. Under flexible rate of exchange, in case of adverse BOP, rate of exchange goes down automatically, as a result, export will increase and adverse BOP will be corrected

4. **Exchange control**

Central Bank of the country exclusively controls the use of foreign exchange. Without the permission of RBI foreign exchange is not made available to anyone. Thus, imports are restricted and controlled under this method and balance of payments of the country is corrected.

5. **Import Duties**

To discourage imports, their value is raised by levying new import duties. In this way, imports become dearer but their demand also goes down and consequently adverse BOP will be corrected

6. **Export Promotion**

By raising the export, adverse BOP will be corrected. All duties and restriction should be withdrawn and export industries be given special concession and facilities. Intensively publicity and advertisement should be undertaken to increase the demand for domestic product in foreign countries

7. **Encouragement to Foreign investment**

Investment of foreign capital in the county constitutes a credit item and so has a favourable effect on the balance of payment position

8. **Attraction to foreign tourists**

In order to attract tourists, government has to develop recreation parks and entertainment programs. Foreign tourists bring along with them large amount of foreign currency which serves the same purpose as the exports

9. **Changes in Basis political Ideology**

Changes in basis ideologies like, socialism, capitalism, nationalism etc. also help correct an adverse balance of payments

10. **Social measures**

Balance of Payment can be corrected through the medium of social psychology. Awakening of swadeshi spirit had adversely affected the BOP of British India. Presently import of petrol and petroleum product is one the major causes of adverse balance of payment of India. If social awareness is aroused the people to make economical use of petrol, it will have a salutary effect on the balance of payment

Trends in Balance of Payments of India

India initiated economic reforms to find the way out of the growing crisis. Structural measures emphasized accelerating the process of industrial and import delicensing and then shifted to further trade liberalization, financial sector reform and tax reform. Prior to 1991, capital flows to India predominately consisted of aid flows, commercial borrowings, and nonresident Indian deposits. Direct investment was restricted, foreign portfolio investment was channeled almost exclusively into a small number of public sector bond issues, and foreign equity holdings in Indian companies were not permitted (Chopra and others, 1995). However, this development strategy of both inward-looking and highly interventionist, consisting of import protection, complex industrial licensing requirements etc underwent radical changes with the liberalization policies of 1991. The post reform period really eased India's struggles with regard to external sector.

vajiramias.com

This is evident from the RBI data summarizing the BOP in current account and capital account. The current account which measures all transactions including exports and imports of goods and services, income receivable and payable abroad, and current transfers from and to abroad remained almost negative throughout the post reform period except for the three financial years. Until 2000-01, the current account deficit that comprises both trade balance and the invisible balance, remained stagnant and stood around $ 5000 million. However, for the first time since 1991, the current account recorded surplus in its account during three consecutive financial years 2 from 2001-02. The deficit in current account continued to occur from 2004-05 onwards and the growth rate was comparatively faster. Surprisingly, the current account deficit grew like anything since 2007-08, the period witnessed financial crisis. The current account balance of India during 2011-12 is recorded to be $ - 78155 million, signifying a deficit eight times that of the figures of 2007-08. Huge negative debits and comparatively low positive credits caused for this negative value in current account. Another notable feature of current account balance is that the deficit was mounting during the previous years. Two major items of current account are merchandise and the invisibles. These two items generate the value of current account balance of the country. The net merchandise has been always found to be huge negative figure. During 2011-12 it was recorded to be $ - 189759 million. During the same period, our total merchandise credit was $ 309774 million while our merchandise debit was $ 499533 million. This is a common feature of India's merchandise figures during all the years. The recent crisis of 2008 affected the trade performance of India in a large way. Indian economy had been growing robustly at an annual average rate of 8.8 per cent for the period 2003-04 to 2007-08. Concerned by the inflationary pressures, Reserve Bank of India (RBI) increased the interest rates, which resulted in a slowdown of India's trade flows prior to the Lehman crisis (Kumar and Alex, 2009). The trade flows, which are one of the important channels through which India was affected during the recent global crisis of 2008, started to collapse from late 2008. Merchandise trade, software exports and remittances declined in absolute terms in response to the exogenous external shock.

INDIA'S BALANCE OF PAYMENTS ON CURRENT ACCOUNT

(₹ Crore)

Period	Trade Deficit	Net Invisibles	Balance of Payments
First Plan	-542	500	-42
Second Plan	-2339	614	-1725
Third Plan	-2382	431	-1951
Annual Plan	-2067	+ 52	-2015
Fourth Plan	-1564	+ 1664	100
Fifth Plan	-3179	+ 6221	+ 3082
Sixth Plan	-30456	+ 19072	-11384
Seventh Plan	- 54204	+ 13157	-41047
Eigth Plan	-149001	+ 86572	-62429
Ninth Plan	N.A	N.A	–62715
Tenth Plan	N.A	N.A	–46343
Eleventh Plan (2010-11)	N.A	N.A	–2,10,100

Source : RBI Bulletin April 2012.

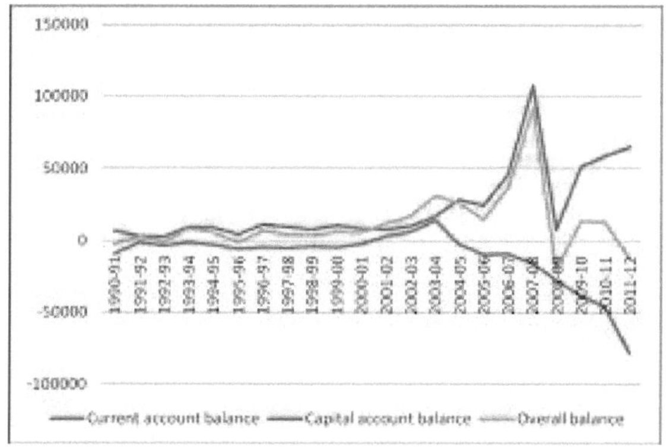

mpra.ub.uni-muenchen.de

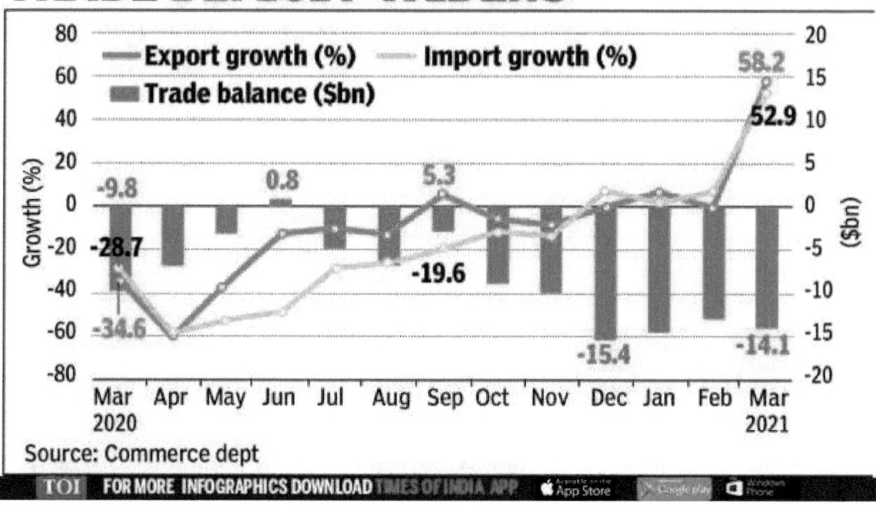

insightsonindia.com

Causes of deterioration in India's balance of payments (BOP) during 1990 and 1991 and Measures did the government take to overcome the crisis

Causes of deterioration

The Balance of Payments (BOP) is the net outcome of current and capital accounts of any economy. The causes for deterioration in India's BOP, in the 1990s are due to:

1.**Persian gulf war**

a. led to Increase in global oil prices which India imports 70% of its total consumption.

b. Indian expatriate workers- nearly 1,00,000 workers- migrated back to India curtails remittance inflows.

2.**Domestic economy**

a. Import of large number of essential commodities - rice, wheat, pulses - due to supply side constraints - lack of agricultural productivity, irrigation infrastructure, transportation costs, leakage

b. Import of manufactured products due to license raj, over regulation that avoided industries from producing diversified products.

Measures taken:

1. **Devaluation of rupee**

a. large foreign investment inflows.

b. Increased exports

2. **Liberalization reforms**

a. opened many sectors - telecommunications, information technology, aviation, banking services - to private sector.

b. foreign investment in equity markets, FDI

3. **Issuance of govt bonds**

a. many foreign companies bought external bonds anticipating good returns

4. **Structural reforms**

a. increase investment in agriculture

b. exports increased and competitive in prices

The newly formed govt under Narshima Rao and then Finance minister Dr. Manmohan Singh's long-term economic vision and political will helped in bringing India out of the financial crisis and made India move away from so called 'Hindu' growth rate of 3% to 5-6%.

CHAPTER V

Demand Analysis and Theory of Production

Introduction

What is Demand Function?

Demand Function is the relationship between the quantity demanded and the price of the commodity.

Mathematically, a function is a symbolic representation of the relationship between dependent and independent variables.

Demand function represents the relationship between the quantity demanded for a commodity (dependent variable) and the price of the commodity (independent variable).

Let us assume that the quantity demanded of a commodity X is Dx, which depends only on its price Px, while other factors are constant. It can be mathematically represented as:

$Dx = f\ (Px)$

However, the quantitative relationship between Dx and Px is expressed as:

$Dx = a - bPx$

Where, a (intercept) and b (relationship between Dx and Px) are constants.

Types of Demand Function

2 types of demand function are:

- Linear demand function
- Non-linear demand function

Linear demand function

In the linear demand function, the slope of the demand curve remains constant throughout its length. A linear demand equation is mathematically expressed as:

$Dx = a - bPx$

In this equation, a denotes the total demand at zero price.

b = slope or the relationship between Dx and Px

b can also be denoted by change in Dx for change in Px

If the values of a and b are known, the demand for a commodity at any given price can be computed using the equation given above.

For example, let us assume a = 50, b = 2.5, and Px= 10:

Demand function is:

Dx = 50 – 2.5 (Px Therefore, Dx = 50 – 2.5 (10)

or Dx= 25 units

The demand schedule for the above function is given in Table

QUANTITY DEMANDED OF COMMODITY X	PRICE LEVELS OF COMMODITY X
5	18
10	16
15	14
20	12

When the demand schedule is plotted on a graph, it produces a linear demand curve, which is shown in Figure below.

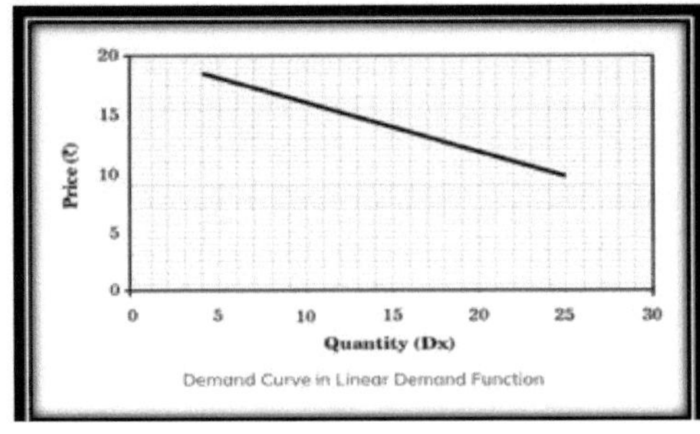

Demand Curve in Linear Demand Function

Non-linear demand function

In the non-linear or curvilinear demand function, the slope of the demand curve (ΔP/ΔQ) changes along the demand curve. Instead of a demand line, non-linear demand function yields a demand curve.

A non-linear demand equation is mathematically expressed as:

Dx = a (Px)-b

Or of a rectangular hyperbola of the form

Dx = (a/Px + c) b

where a, b, c> 0

Exponent –b of price in the non-linear demand function refers to the coefficient of the price elasticity of demand.

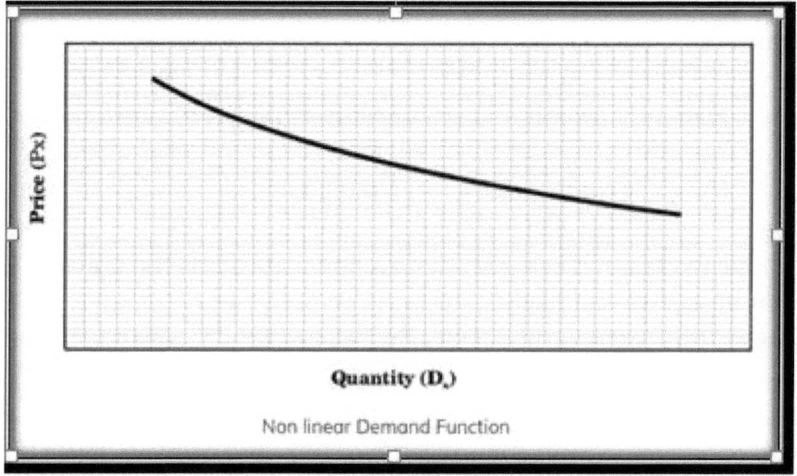

Non linear Demand Function

Figure, represents a non-linear demand function:

Determinants of Demand with Examples and Formula

Demand drives economic growth. Businesses want to increase demand so they can improve profits. Governments and central banks boost demand to end recessions. They slow it during the expansion phase of the business cycle to combat inflation. If you offer any paid services, then you are trying to raise demand for them.

So what drives demand? In the real world, a potentially infinite number of factors impact each consumer's decision to buy something. In economics, however, the equation is simplified to highlight the five primary determinants of individual demand and a sixth for aggregate demand.

The Five Determinants of Demand

The five determinants of demand are:

- The price of the good or service.
- The income of buyers.
- The prices of related goods or services—either complementary and purchased along with a particular item, or substitutes and bought instead of a product.
- The tastes or preferences of consumers will drive demand.

- Consumer expectations. Most often, this refers to whether a consumer believes prices for the product will rise or fall in the future.

For aggregate demand, the number of buyers in the market is the sixth determinant.

Demand Equation or Function

This equation expresses the relationship between demand and its five determinants

qD = f (price, income, prices of related goods, tastes, expectations)

As you can see, this isn't a straightforward equation like 2 + 2 = 4. It isn't that simple to create an equation that accurately predicts the exact quantity that consumers will demand.

Instead, this equation highlights the relationship between demand and its key factors. The quantity demanded (qD) is a function of five factors—price, buyer income, the price of related goods, consumer tastes, and any consumer expectations of future supply and price. As these factors change, so too does the quantity demanded.

How Each Determinant Affects Demand

Each factor's impact on demand is unique. When the income of the buyer increases, for example, that could also increase demand. The buyer has more money and is more likely to spend it. But when other factors increase—like the price of related goods, for example—demand could decrease.

Before breaking down the effect of each determinant, it's important to note that these factors don't change in a vacuum. All the factors are in flux all the time. To understand how one determinant affects demand, you must first hypothetically assume that all the other determinants don't change.1

That principle is called ceteris paribus or "all other things being equal." So, "ceteris paribus," here's how each element affects demand.

1. **Price**

The law of demand states that when prices rise, the quantity of demand falls. That also means that when prices drop, demand will grow. People base their purchasing decisions on price if all other things are equal. The exact quantity bought for each price level is described in the demand schedule. It's then plotted on a graph to show the demand curve.

The demand curve shows just the relationship between price and quantity. If one of the other determinants changes, the entire demand curve shifts.

If the quantity demanded responds a lot to price, then it's known as elastic demand. If demand doesn't change much, regardless of price, that's inelastic demand.

1. **Income**

When income rises, so will the quantity demanded. When income falls, so will demand. But if your income doubles, you won't always buy twice as much of a particular good or service. There's only so many pints of ice cream you'd want to eat, no matter how wealthy you are, and this is an example of "marginal utility."

Marginal utility is the concept that each unit of a good or service is a little less useful to you than the first. At some point, you won't want it anymore, and the marginal utility drops to zero.

The first pint of ice cream tastes delicious. You might have another. But after that, the marginal utility starts to decrease to the point where you don't want any more.

3. **Prices of related goods or services**

The price of complementary goods or services raises the cost of using the product you demand, so you'll want less. For example, when gas prices rose to $4 a gallon in 2008, the demand for gas-guzzling trucks and SUVs fell.2 Gas is a complementary good to these vehicles. The cost of driving a truck rose along with gas prices.

The opposite reaction occurs when the price of a substitute rises. When that happens, people will want more of the good or service and less of its substitute. That's why Apple continually innovates with its iPhones and iPods. As soon as a substitute, such as a new Android phone, appears at a lower price, Apple comes out with a better product. Then the Android is no longer a substitute.

4. **Tastes**

When the public's desires, emotions, or preferences change in favor of a product, so does the quantity demanded. Likewise, when tastes go against it, that depresses the amount demanded. Brand advertising tries to increase the desire for consumer goods.

5. **Expectations**

When people expect that the value of something will rise, they demand more of it. That helps explains the housing asset bubble of 2005. Housing prices rose, but people kept buying houses because they expected the price to continue to increase. Prices continued increasing until the bubble burst in 2007. New home prices fell 22% from their peak of $262,200 in March 2007 to $204,200 in October 2010.3 However, the quantity demanded didn't increase—even as the price decreased—and sales fell from a peak of 1.2 million in 2005 to a low of 306,000 in 2011.4

So why didn't the quantity demanded increase as the price fell? It's in part because the broader economy was experiencing a recession. People expected prices to continue falling, so they didn't feel an urgency to buy a home. Record levels of foreclosures entered the market due to the subprime mortgage crisis. Demand for homes didn't increase until people expected future home prices would, too.

6. **Number of buyers in the market**

The number of consumers affects overall, or "aggregate," demand. As more buyers enter the market, demand rises. That's true even if prices don't change, and the U.S. saw this during the housing bubble of 2005. Low-cost and sub-prime mortgages increased the number of people who could afford a house.5 The total number of buyers in the market expanded. This increased demand for housing. When housing prices started to fall, many realized they couldn't afford their mortgages. At that point, they foreclosed. That reduced the number of buyers and drove down demand.

Elasticity of Demand

Introduction

Demand for a good is said to be "elastic" if a small change in price causes people to demand a lot more or a lot less of the good. Demand for a good is "inelastic" if a small change in prices causes people to make no change or almost no change in how much they demand of that good.

If the price of gasoline at the pump rises, the amount of gas people demand falls. But, does it fall by a lot or only by a little? The price elasticity of demand is all about answering that question. If a 10% increase in the price of gas results in almost no change in the amount of gas people want to buy, we say the price elasticity of demand for gas is inelastic. If it results in a very large reduction in the amount of gas they want to buy, we say the price elasticity of demand for gas is elastic.

Usually economists describe demand as either relatively elastic or relatively inelastic when compared to an imaginary neutral amount of elasticity. That is, if a 10% increase in price results in a 10% decrease in the amount of the good demanded, we think of that as a neutral elasticity of demand. If we know demand for gas is relatively inelastic, we can estimate that when the price of gas goes up by 10% people will not change their buying habits very much, buying almost the same amount of gas as before–that is, reducing their gas purchases by less than 10%. If we know demand for gas is relatively elastic, we can estimate that a 10% increase in the price of gas will cause the quantity of gas demanded at the pump to fall by over 10%.

The price elasticity of demand often depends on how long a time period is involved. The day after the price of gas falls, people may not change their gas purchases or driving habits very much. Perhaps their tanks are already full enough to get where they have already planned to go. But within a week or a month, people will notice that the fall in the price of gas now enables them to travel a little more than they'd previously planned, or relax their daily driving habits and not worry so much about driving to get groceries weekly instead of every other week. That is, after a week or a month, the price elasticity of demand may increase and eventually may settle in at a new level. It is also possible for people to overreact to a price change.

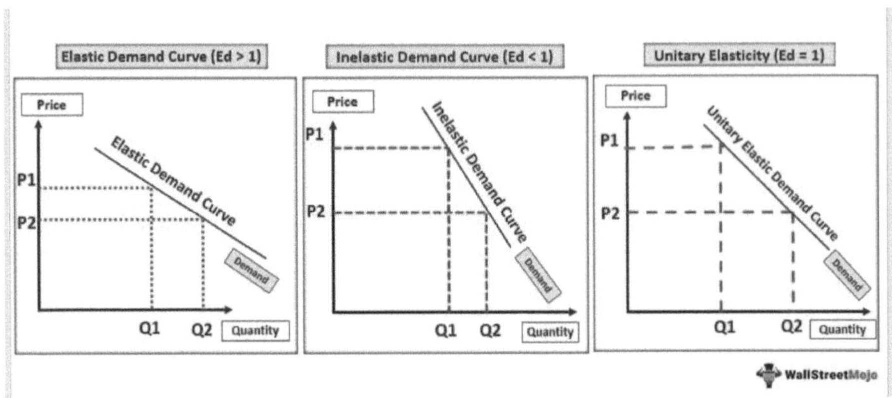

wallstreetmojo.com

The price elasticity of demand often depends on how long a time period is involved. The day after the price of gas falls, people may not change their gas purchases or driving habits very much. Perhaps their tanks are already full enough to get where they have already planned to go. But within a week or a month, people will notice that the fall in the price of gas now enables them to travel a little more than they'd previously planned, or relax their daily driving habits and not worry so much about driving to get groceries weekly instead of every other week. That is, after a week or a month, the price elasticity of demand may increase and eventually may settle in at a new level. It is also possible for people to overreact to a price change.

For example, perhaps people fear that the price will rise again soon and they will lose out on an opportunity. That is, the price elasticity of demand probably changes over time, before settling down. It often takes more time for people to adjust to a sudden, unexpected price change than to a price change they expected because they have more time to rethink their plans when price changes are predicted or announced in advance.

A change in the price of a commodity affects its demand. We can find the elasticity of demand, or the degree of responsiveness of demand by comparing the percentage price changes with the quantities demanded.

The variables on which demand can depend on are :-

- Price of the commodity
- Prices of related commodities

- Consumer's income etc.

Let's look at some examples:-

a. The price of a radio falls from Rs. 500 to Rs. 400 per unit. As a result, the demand increases from 100 to 150 units.
b. Due to government subsidy, the price of wheat falls from Rs.10/kg to Rs.9/kg. Due to this, the demand increases from 500 kilograms to 520 kilograms.

Types of Elasticity of Demand:-

- **Price Elasticity:-** The price elasticity of demand is the response of the quantity demanded to change in the price of a commodity. It is assumed that the consumer's income, tastes and prices of all other goods are steady. It is measured as a percentage change in the quantity demanded divided by the percentage change in price Therefore,

$$\text{price Elasticity} = E_p = \frac{\text{percentage change in quantity demanded}}{\text{percentage change in price}}$$

Ep=Change in Quantity×100Original QuantityChange in Price×100Original Price

=Change in QuantityOriginal Quantity×Original PriceChange in Price

- **Income Elasticity:-** The income elasticity of demand is the degree of responsiveness of the quality demanded to a change in the consumer's income. Symbolically,

EL=Percentage change in quantity demanded Percentage change in income

Cross Elasticity:- The cross elasticity of demand of a commodity X for another commodity Y, is the change in demand of commodity X due to a change in the price of commodity Y. Symbolically,

Where, E_d is the cross elasticity, Δq_x is the original demand of commodity X, Δq_x is the change in demand of X, Δp_y is the original price of commodity Y, and Δp_y is the change in price of Y.

Demand Forecasting & Estimation

No business owner has a crystal ball showing what customers will want during the upcoming year and how much of it they will buy. Fortunately, you can forecast demand using tools and information. While your demand estimation is unlikely to ever be completely accurate, it will still provide you with valuable benchmarks to help you plan. You can estimate and forecast demand using sophisticated mathematical tools based on sampling your entire industry, identifying trends and variables, and applying formulas developed by experts. If your business is smaller and you have access to less data, you can still make projections and plan upcoming production based on observations you have made about your own operations and the ways that demand for your product have trended over time.

Business enterprise needs to know the demand for its product. An existing unit must know current demand for its product in order to avoid underproduction or over production. The current demand should be known for determining pricing and promotion policies so that it is able to secure optimum sales or maximum profit. Demand Estimation is the process of finding current values of demand for various values of prices and other determining variables.

Steps in Demand Estimation:-

1. Identification of independent variables such as price, price of substitutes population, percapita income, advertisement expenditure etc.
2. Collection of data on the variables form past records, publications of various agencies etc.
3. Development a mathematical model or equation that indicates the relationship between independent values of the parameters of the model.
4. Estimation of the parameters of the model i.e, to estimate the unknown values of the parameters of the model.
5. Development of estimates based on the model.

Tools and techniques for demand estimation includes:-

1. Consumer surveys.
2. Consumer clinics and focus groups
3. Market Experiment
4. Statistical techniques.

- **What is Demand Forecasting:-**

Accurate demand forecasting is essential for a firm to enable it to produce the required quantities at the right time and to arrange well in advance for the various factors of production. Forecasting helps the firm to assess the probable demand for its products and plan its production accordingly.

Demand Forecasting refers to an estimate of future demand for the product. It is an objective assessment of the future course of demand. It is essential to distinguish to distinguish between forecast of demand and forecast of sales.

Levels of Demand Function:-

1. **Micro Level:-** Micro level demand forecasting is related to the business conditions prevailing in the economy as a whole.
2. **Industry Level:-** It is prepared by different trade association in order to estimate the demand for particular industries products. Industry includes number of firms. It is useful for inter- industry comparison.
3. **Firm Level:-** It is more important from managerial view point as it helps the management in decision making with regard to the firms demand and production.

Types of Demand Forecasting:-

- **Short term Demand Forecasting:-** Short term Demand forecasting is limited to short periods. Usually for one year. Important purposes of short term demand forecasting are given below:-

1. Making a suitable production policy to avoid over production or under production.

2. Helping the firm to reduce the cost of purchasing raw materials and to control inventory.
3. Deciding suitable price policy so as to avoid an increase when the demand is low.
4. Forecasting short term financial requirements for planned production.

- **Long term Demand Forecasting:-** This forecasting is meant for long period. The important purpose of long term forecasting is given below:-

1. Planning of a new unit or expansion of existing on them basis of analysis of long term potential of the product demand.
2. Planning long term financial requirements on the basis of long term sales forecasting.
3. Planning of manpower requirements can be made on the basis of long term sales forecast.
4. To forecast future problems of material supply and energy crisis.

Difference Between Estimation and Forecasting

Although estimation and forecasting are processes that are often used together, they aren't the same. Estimation looks for links between data and operations, finding the reasons behind the numbers and using this information to plan for the future. Forecasting is driven by numbers rather than stories. It issues predictions based on past records without necessarily delving into why certain patterns have occurred. An estimation process for a weather dependent business such as a food concession could start with identifying the effects that sun, clouds and rain have on daily sales, and then researching the average number of sunny, cloudy and rainy days per year. A forecasting model could simply look at average sales during a particular month or season over several previous years. It would then factor in developments such as new products being introduced. This information would provide the basis for forecasting sales during an upcoming period.

Importance of Estimation and Forecasting

Your business will use the information you get from estimation and forecasting to plan production and inventory. This is especially important if your production process requires considerable lead time to obtain parts from manufacturers and perform a series of interdependent tasks. If your estimation is faulty and your forecasting is too high, you may lose money by ending up with excess inventory that you can't use. If your forecast falls short of demand, you may lose money by receiving orders that you can't fill. Apart from the immediate sales lost, this situation could also hurt your business by making potential customers reluctant to order from you in the future. A business with a shorter production cycle will be better able to adjust for a shortfall caused by a faulty forecast by scrambling and producing extra, but you'll probably pay extra for parts ordered in small quantities on short notice. Your payroll may also increase because last minute orders often require overtime hours.

Variables Affecting Demand Forecasting

Although countless variables will affect the demand for your product, you won't be able to include them all in your forecasting model. Demand for bottled water spikes during natural disasters but these events are notoriously hard to predict. Despite these difficulties, the better you get at identifying trends and correlations that affect consumer demand, the better your estimations and forecasts will be.

Marketing and advertising drive demand. If you've conducted successful campaigns in the past and you consistently get a good response to your marketing efforts, it's reasonably safe to forecast increases in sales to correspond with advertising expenditures. If your business experiences seasonal fluctuations that are weather dependent needs for your products, you can use sales figures from previous years to estimate current demand. If you manufacture windshield ice scrapers, it's safe to say that you'll sell more in the winter than in the summer.

Some variables are easier to predict in the short term than in the long term. It's tricky to try to estimate, based on overall economic climate or fashion trends when you're looking five years into the future. It's safer to base longer term forecasts on variables that you can predict and influence, than on global developments that are completely beyond your control.

Theory of Production Function

Production Function

The production function relates the maximum amount of output that can be obtained from a given number of inputs.

What Is Theory Of Production:

In economics, production theory explains the principles in which the business has to take decisions on how much of each commodity it sells and how much it produces and also how much of raw material ie., fixed capital and labor it employs and how much it will use. It defines the relationships between the prices of the commodities and productive factors on one hand

and the quantities of these commodities and productive factors that are produced on the other hand.

Production is a process of combining various inputs to produce an output for consumption. It is the act of creating output in the form of a commodity or a service that contributes to the utility of individuals.

In other words, it is a process in which the inputs are converted into outputs.

the Production function signifies a technical relationship between the physical inputs and physical outputs of the firm, for a given state of the technology.

Q = f (a, b, c, ... z)

Where a,b,c ....z are various inputs such as land, labor ,capital etc. Q is the level of the output for a firm.

If labor (L) and capital (K) are only the input factors, the production function reduces to –

Q = f(L, K)

Production Function describes the technological relationship between inputs and outputs. It is a tool that analysis the qualitative input – output relationship and also represents the technology of a firm or the economy as a whole.

Define the production function

Key Points

- The production function describes a boundary or frontier representing the limit of output obtainable from each feasible combination of inputs.
- Firms use the production function to determine how much output they should produce given the price of a good, and what combination of inputs they should use to produce given the price of capital and labor.
- The production function also gives information about increasing or decreasing returns to scale and the marginal products of labor and capital.

Key Terms

1. **Production function**

Relates physical output of a production process to physical inputs or factors of production.

1. **Marginal cost**

The increase in cost that accompanies a unit increase in output; the partial derivative of the cost function with respect to output. Additional cost associated with producing one more unit of output.

3. **Output**

Production; quantity produced, created, or completed.

In economics, a production function relates physical output of a production process to physical inputs or factors of production. It is a mathematical function that relates the maximum amount of output that can be obtained from a given number of inputs – generally capital and labor. The production function, therefore, describes a boundary or frontier representing the limit of output obtainable from each feasible combination of inputs.

Firms use the production function to determine how much output they should produce given the price of a good, and what combination of inputs they should use to produce given the price of capital and labor. When firms are deciding how much to produce they typically find that at high levels of production, their marginal costs begin increasing. This is also known as diminishing returns to scale – increasing the quantity of inputs creates a less-than-proportional increase in the quantity of output. If it weren't for diminishing returns to scale, supply could expand without limits without increasing the price of a good.

4. **Factory Production**

Manufacturing companies use their production function to determine the optimal combination of labor and capital to produce a certain amount of output.

Increasing marginal costs can be identified using the production function. If a firm has a production function $Q=F(K,L)$ (that is, the quantity of output (Q) is some function of capital (K) and labor (L)), then if $2Q<F(2K,2L)$, the production function has increasing marginal costs and diminishing returns to scale. Similarly, if $2Q>F(2K,2L)$, there are increasing returns to scale, and if $2Q=F(2K,2L)$, there are constant returns to scale.

Examples of Common Production Functions

One very simple example of a production function might be Q=K+L, where Q is the quantity of output, K is the amount of capital, and L is the amount of labor used in production. This production function says that a firm can produce one unit of output for every unit of capital or labor it employs. From this production function we can see that this industry has constant returns to scale – that is, the amount of output will increase proportionally to any increase in the amount of inputs.

Another common production function is the Cobb-Douglas production function. One example of this type of function is Q=K0.5L0.5. This describes a firm that requires the least total number of inputs when the combination of inputs is relatively equal. For example, the firm could produce 25 units of output by using 25 units of capital and 25 of labor, or it could produce the same 25 units of output with 125 units of labor and only one unit of capital.

Finally, the Leontief production function applies to situations in which inputs must be used in fixed proportions; starting from those proportions, if usage of one input is increased without another being increased, output will not change. This production function is given by Q=Min(K,L). For example, a firm with five employees will produce five units of output as long as it has at least five units of capital.

Difference Between Short Run and Long Run Production Function

A short-run production function refers to that period of time, in which the installation of new plant and machinery to increase the production level is not possible. On the other hand, the Long-run production function is one in which the firm has got sufficient time to instal new machinery or capital equipment, instead of increasing the labour units.

The production function can be described as the operational relationship between the inputs and outputs, in the sense that the maximum amount of finished goods that can be produced with the given factors of production, under a particular state of technical knowledge. There are two kinds of the production function, short run production function and long run production function.

Applications Of Demand Analysis In Managerial Decision Making:

There is great importance of demand analysis for any businesses activity. So, the study demand analysis is very essential for any rational entrepreneur before starting a business because the objective would be the maximization for profit with efficient allocation of limited resources. The demand analysis helps the entrepreneur in taking decisions for the efficient allocation of limited resources.

- **Forecasting of necessity:-** Demand analysis makes it easy for the entrepreneur to know about the kinds of goods necessary in the market or society. With this the entrepreneur can easily find out the type of goods to be produced for the maximization of the profit beforehand. For this, the income of consumers, tastes, desire, fashions etc. Should be looked upon very carefully.
- **Sale Forecasting:-** Any entrepreneur has to produce the goods in respect to the sales estimation. For sales forecasting also the demand analysis is of great importance. Entrepreneur will be successful if goods are produced by estimating the prior to production with the help of demand analysis. Entrepreneur will be successful if production is carried out only after the full study of market demand. So, with the help of demand analysis it will be easier for the entrepreneur to decide the quantity of goods to be produced.
- **Price determination:-** Demand analysis plays an important role in price determination also because price is the main determinant for that effects the demand. So, it is necessary for any entrepreneur to study demand analysis prior to price determination. Goods consumed by the consumers are not of same types, some are luxurious goods and some are necessities. So, demand analysis plays an important role in the price determination of different types of goods.
- **Decision relating to profit:-** Every entrepreneur has to decide very carefully when determining the profit because the products are of various types. Government will interface if the price level of the essential goods becomes high. So, with the help of demand analysis essential goods and luxurious goods should be categorized and price accordingly. For the categorizing of different goods demand analysis is very essential for the entrepreneurs.
- **Financial provision:-** Every entrepreneur will run the businesses with the financial provisions. So the make a decision of the financial provision required to run a business's there is a necessity of demand analysis. A business will be successful if financial provision is fulfilled according to demand analysis.

There is a great importance of demand analysis in carrying out various businesses activities. Any entrepreneur has to formulate businesses policies according to demand analysis, otherwise might be a failure.

Comparison Chart

Difference between Short Run and Long Run Production Function

Basis of Difference	Short-Run Production Function	Long-Run Production Function
Meaning	It defines the functional relationship between inputs and output of a commodity for a short period of time.	It defines the functional relationship between inputs and output of a commodity for a longer period of time.
Also known as	It is also known as Variable proportion type of production function.	It is also known as a fixed proportion type of production function.
Capital-Labour Ratio	In this, the capital-labour ratio changes with the change in output.	In this, the capital-labour ratio doesn't change with the change in output.
Related Law	The law of returns to a factor is applied for this function.	The law of returns to a scale is applied for this function.
Curve	The curve of the short-run production function is parallel to the horizontal axis.	The curve of the long-run production function is upward sloping.
Fixed and Variable Factors	Here, the capital is assumed as the fixed factor and labour as a variable factor.	Here, all the factors of production are variable factors.
Scale of Production	There is no change in the scale of production in the short run.	Here, The scale of production is always changed with a change in output.
Entry and Exit of Firms	In this, there are barriers for firms to enter and to shut down but cant exit.	In this, the firms are free to enter and exit the market.

tutorstips.com

Short Run Production Function

The short run production function is one in which at least is one factor of production is thought to be fixed in supply, i.e. it cannot be increased or decreased, and the rest of the factors are variable in nature.

In general, the firm's capital inputs are assumed as fixed, and the production level can be changed by changing the quantity of other inputs such as labour, raw material, capital and so on. Therefore, it is quite difficult for the firm to change the capital equipment, to increase the output produced, among all factors of production.

In such circumstances, the law of variable proportion or laws of returns to variable input operates, which states the consequences when extra units of a variable input are combined with a fixed input. In short run, increasing returns are due to the indivisibility of factors and specialisation, whereas diminishing returns is due to the perfect elasticity of substitution of factors.

Long Run Production Function

Long run production function refers to that time period in which all the inputs of the firm are variable. It can operate at various activity levels because the firm can change and adjust all the factors of production and level of output produced according to the business environment. So, the firm has the flexibility of switching between two scales.

In such a condition, the law of returns to scale operates which discusses, in what way, the output varies with the change in production level, i.e. the relationship between the activity level and the quantities of output. The increasing returns to scale is due to the economies of scale and decreasing returns to scale is due to the diseconomies of scale.

Key Differences Between Short Run and Long Run Production Function

The difference between short run and long run production function can be drawn clearly as follows:

- The short run production function can be understood as the time period over which the firm is not able to change the quantities of all inputs. Conversely, long run production function indicates the time period, over which the firm can change the quantities of all the inputs.
- While in short run production function, the law of variable proportion operates, in the long-run production function, the law of returns to scale operates.
- The activity level does not change in the short run production function, whereas the firm can expand or reduce the activity levels in the long run production function.
- In short run production function the factor ratio changes because one input varies while the remaining are fixed in nature. As opposed, the factor proportion remains same in the long run production function, as all factor inputs vary in the same proportion.
- In short run, there are barriers to the entry of firms, as well as the firms can shut down but cannot exit. On the contrary, firms are free to enter and exit in the long run.

Conclusion

To sum up, the production function is nothing but a mathematical presentation of technological input-output relationship.

For any production function, short run simply means a shorter time period than the long run. So, for different processes, the definition of the long run and short run varies, and so one cannot indicate the two time periods in days, months or years. These can only be understood by looking whether all the inputs are variable or not.

The Law of Diminishing Returns

The law of diminishing returns states that adding more of one factor of production will at some point yield lower per-unit returns.

The law of diminishing returns is an economic principle stating that as investment in a particular area increases, the rate of profit from that investment, after a certain point, cannot continue to increase if other variables remain at a constant. As investment continues past that point, the return diminishes progressively.

For example, the law of diminishing returns states that in a production process, adding more workers might initially increase output and eventually creates the optimal output per worker. After that optimal point, however, the efficiency of each worker decreases because other factors -- such as the production technique or the available resources -- remain the same (this is known, more specifically, as the law of diminishing marginal returns). This kind of problem might be addressed by modernizing the production technique using technology.

The law of diminishing returns in the real world

While the law of diminishing returns originated in classic economic theory, it is one of the most widely recognized economic principles outside the economics classroom. Some of the most common examples relate to farming, but the law applies in many other real-world situations that extend beyond production and manufacturing into realms such as marketing and customer relationship management.

A good example is social media marketing endeavors. While it is tempting to think that doubling the budget on a social media marketing campaign will double the returns, the increase could easily lead to a glut on information on a single social media channel, causing the returns to decrease substantially. To address this problem, a marketing department should evaluate and adjust other variables, such as its chosen channels or its approach to social media monitoring and analytics.

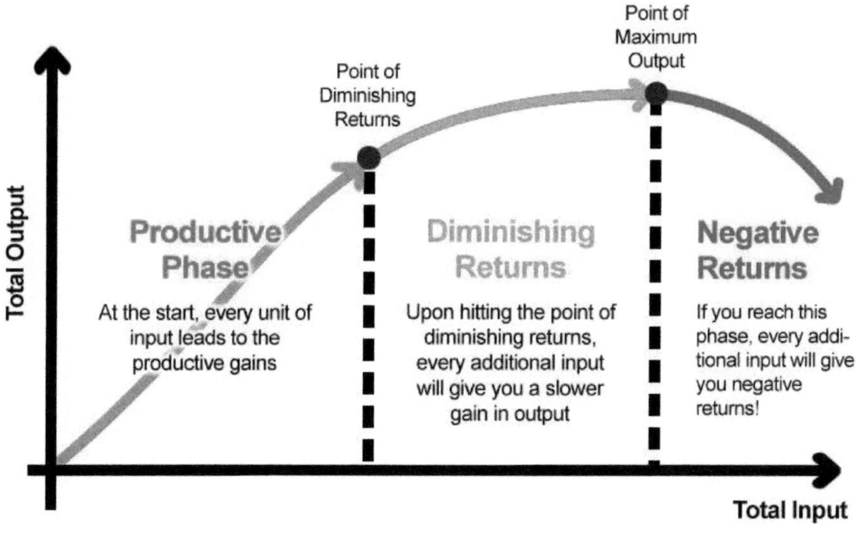

personalexcellence.co

To stay competitive in areas from campaign planning to enterprise resource planning, it's also important that organizations establish the point of diminishing returns -- which is when per-unit returns start to drop.

To do this, organizations can define the single resource they plan to increase: the number of agents in a call center, for example. Next, they define the total cost of the desired output. This formula becomes trickier, as the output runs the risk of moving from defined numbers to more amorphous metrics such as customer satisfaction.

Key Points

One consequence of the law of diminishing returns is that producing one more unit of output will eventually cost increasingly more, due to inputs being used less and less effectively.

The marginal cost curve will initially be downward sloping, representing added efficiency as production increases. If the law of diminishing returns holds, however, the marginal cost curve will eventually slope upward and continue to rise.

The SRAC is typically U-shaped with its minimum at the point where it intersect the marginal cost curve. This is caused by the first increasing, and then decreasing, marginal returns to labor.

The typical LRAC curve is also U-shaped, reflecting increasing returns of scale where negatively-sloped, constant returns to scale where horizontal and decreasing returns where positively sloped.

Key Terms

Returns to scale: A term referring to changes in output resulting from a proportional change in all inputs (where all inputs increase by a constant factor).

Marginal cost: The increase in cost that accompanies a unit increase in output; the partial derivative of the cost function with respect to output. Additional cost associated with producing one more unit of output.

A Farmer Example of Diminishing Returns

Consider a corn farmer with one acre of land. In addition to land, other factors include quantity of seeds, fertilizer, water, and labor. Assume the farmer has already decided how much seed, water, and labor he will be using this season. He is still deciding on how much fertilizer to use. As he increases the amount of fertilizer, the output of corn will increase. It may also reach a point where the output actually begins to decrease since too much fertilizer can become poisonous.

The law of diminishing returns states that there will be a point where the additional output of corn gained from one additional unit of fertilizer will be smaller than the additional output of corn from the previous increase in fertilizer. This table shows the output of corn per unit of fertilizer:

1	100	100
2	250	150
3	425	175
4	550	125
5	600	50
6	525	-75

Output of corn per unit fertilizer

As the farmer increases from one to two units of fertilizer, total output increases from 100 to 250 ears of corn. Therefore the marginal, or additional, ears of corn gained from one more unit of fertilizer is 150 (250 - 100). From two to three units of fertilizer, the total output increases from 250 to 425 ears of corn, a 175 marginal increase.

At what point does the law of diminishing returns set in? Look for the point at which the marginal increase is at the highest point and the next marginal increase is less. In this example, that occurs after the farmer adds the third unit of fertilizer. At three units, the marginal output in ears of corn is 175, but when the fourth unit is added, the marginal output drops to 125.

Again, this does not mean the total production starts to decrease. In fact, the total production is still increasing, as shown in the total ears of corn column. Also note that at the sixth unit of fertilizer, the farmer starts to experience negative returns, where the increase in fertilizer actually decreases the total output and the marginal output becomes negative.

In economics, diminishing returns (also called diminishing marginal returns) is the decrease in the marginal output of a production process as the amount of a single factor of production is increased, while the amounts of all other factors of production stay constant. The law of diminishing returns states that in all productive processes, adding more of one factor of production, while holding all others constant ("ceteris paribus"), will at some point yield lower per-unit returns. The law of diminishing returns does not imply that adding more of a factor will decrease the total production, a condition known as negative returns, though in fact, this is common.

CHAPTER VI

Theory of Cost and Market Structures

Introduction

What is Cost?

To an economist, the cost of producing any good or service is its opportunity cost. In everyday living, all man-made choices have alternatives. Therefore the opportunity cost of obtaining a commodity is the foregone utility that could have been derived from the forgone alternatives. Cost is best described as a sacrifice made in order to get something. In business, the cost is usually a monetary valuation of all efforts, materials, resources, time, and utilities consumed, the risk incurred and opportunities forgone in production and delivery of goods and services. More explicitly, the costs attached to resources that a firm uses to produce its product are divided into explicit costs and implicit costs. All expenses are costs but not all costs are expenses. Those costs incurred in the acquisition of income-generating assets are not considered expenses. The theory of costs is better categorized under the traditional and modern theories of cost.

What is implied by the Theory of Cost?

The assurance of the cost for an item or administration is difficult. A few different variables administer it. The hypothesis of cost definition expresses that the expenses of a business exceptionally decide its stock and expenditures. The cutting edge hypothesis of cost in Economics investigates the ideas of cost, short-run aggregate and normal expense, long-run cost alongside economy scales.

The expense work fluctuates concerning variables, for example, activity scale, yield size, cost of creation, and the sky is the limit from there. The hypothesis of cost creation should be perceived exhaustively by financial experts to run their organization and increment its benefit and usefulness.

Theory of Cost in Economics

The advanced hypothesis of cost in Economics likewise determines economies of scale where an expanded creation diminishes the expense per unit of creation. The profits to scale first increment, then, at that point, settle for quite a while and afterward decline. How about we investigate the various kinds of economies-

1. **Specialized:** Technical economies remember speculation for apparatus and more proficient capital gear to expand creation effectiveness.
2. **Powerful Management:** When an association builds activity, they need a superior division of work into different sub-offices for productive administration.
3. **Business:** a lot of parts and unrefined components is required with expanded creation. Thus natural substance costs decline. The commercial expense for a unit of creation likewise falls, which increments.
4. **Finance:** With a raised Finance, any organization becomes famous. Their financial protections increment and Finance is raised at a much lower cost.
5. **Hazard Management:** As the firm turns out to be more different, hazard taking variables likewise increment.

Comparison in the Short and Long Run Costs

According to cost analysis theory, a company tries to increase output in the short run by changing only the variable factors such as raw materials or labour. The fixed variables are left alone. The long-run period is when the company can change any factor in order to obtain desired outputs that align with their goals. All of these factors add up to a cost.

Examples that have been solved

1. Determine the relationship between a company's total cost, total fixed cost, and total variable cost.For any company,

Total Costs (TC) equals Total Fixed Costs (TFC) plus Total Variable Costs (TVC) (TVC).

Traditional and Modern Theory of Cost in Short and Long Runs

The traditional theory distinguishes between the short run and the long run. The short-run is the period during which some factors) is fixed; usually, capital equipment and entrepreneurship are considered fixed in the short run.

The long-run is the period over which all factors become variable.

A. Short-Run Costs of the Traditional Theory:

In the traditional theory of the firm total costs are split into two groups' total fixed costs and total variable costs:

TC = TFC + TVC

The fixed costs include:

(a) Salaries of administrative staff

(b) Depreciation (wear and tear) of machinery

(c) Expenses for building depreciation and repairs

(d) Expenses for land maintenance and depreciation (if any).

Another element that may be treated in the same way as fixed costs is the normal profit, which a lump sum including a percentage return on is fixed capital and allowance for risk.

The variable costs include:

(a) The raw materials

(b) The cost of direct labour

(c) The running expenses of fixed capital, such as fuel, ordinary repairs and routine maintenance.

The total fixed cost is graphically denoted by a straight line parallel to the output axis (figure 4.1). The total variable cost in the traditional theory of the firm has broadly an inverse-S shape (figure 4.2) which reflects the law of variable proportions. According to this law, at the initial stages of production with a given plant, as more of the variable factors) is employed, its productivity increases and the average variable cost falls.

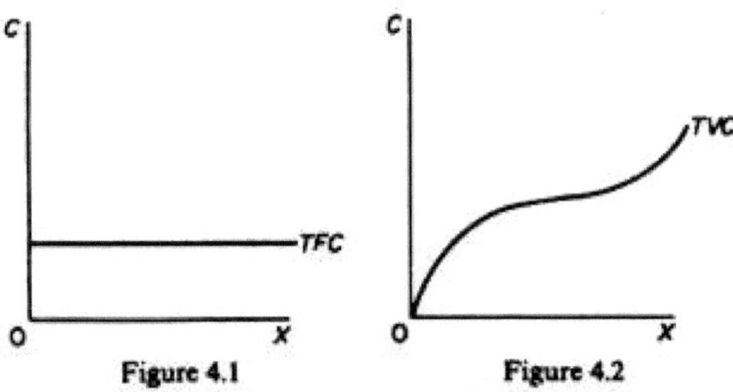

Figure 4.1 Figure 4.2

This continues until the optimal combination of the fixed and variable factors is reached. Beyond this point as increased quantities of the variable factors(s) are combined with the fixed factors) the productivity of the variable factors) declines (and the A VC rises). By adding the TFC and TVC we obtain the TC of the firm (figure 4.3). From the total-cost curves, we obtain average-cost curves.

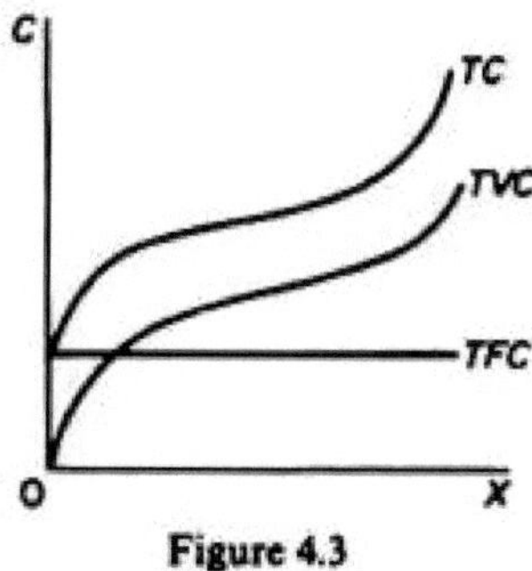

Figure 4.3

The average fixed cost is found by dividing TFC by the level of output:

AFC = TFC / X

Graphically the AFC is a rectangular hyperbola, showing at all its points the same magnitude, that is, the level of TFC (figure 4.4).

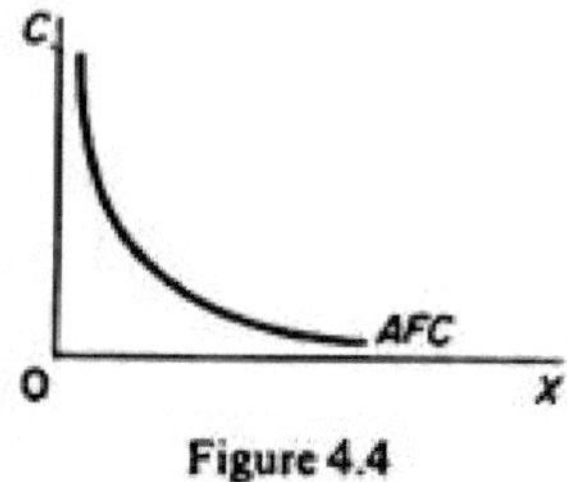

Figure 4.4

The average variable cost is similarly obtained by dividing the TVC with the corresponding level of output:

AVC = TVC / X

Graphically the A VC at each level of output is derived from the slope of a line drawn from the origin to the point on the TVC curve corresponding to the particular level of output. For example, in figure 4.5 the AVC at X_1 is the slope of the ray 0a, the A VC at X_2 is the slope of the ray Ob, and so on. It is clear from figure 4.5 that the slope of a ray through the origin declines continuously until the ray becomes tangent to the TVC curve at c. To the right of this point, the slope of rays through the origin starts increasing. Thus the SA VC curve falls initially as the productivity of the variable factors) increases reach a minimum when the plant is operated optimally (with the optimal combination of fixed and variable factors), and rises beyond that point (figure 4.6).

The ATC is obtained by dividing the TC by the corresponding level of output:

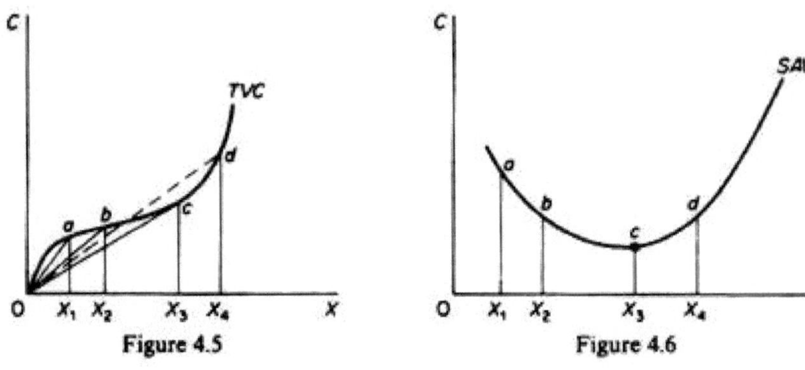

Figure 4.5 Figure 4.6

ATC = TC / X = TFC + TVC / X = AFC + AVC

Graphically the ATC curve is derived in the same way as the SAVC. The ATC at any level of output is the slope of the straight line from the origin to the point on the TC curve corresponding to that particular level of output (figure 4.7). The shape of the A TC is similar to that of the AVC (both being U-shaped). Initially, the ATC declines, it reaches a minimum at the level of optimal operation of the plant (X_M) and subsequently rises again (figure 4.8).

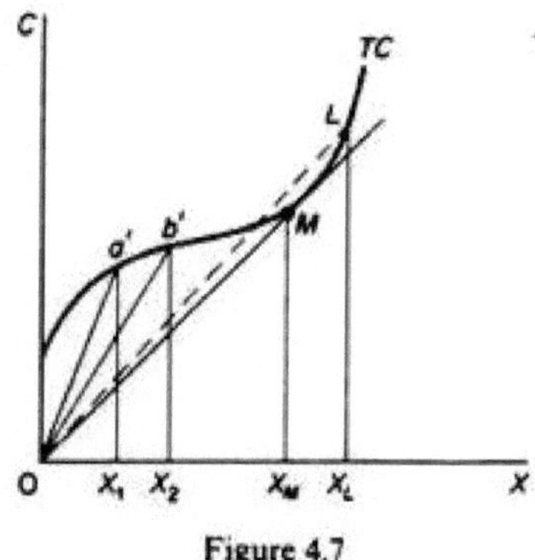

Figure 4.7

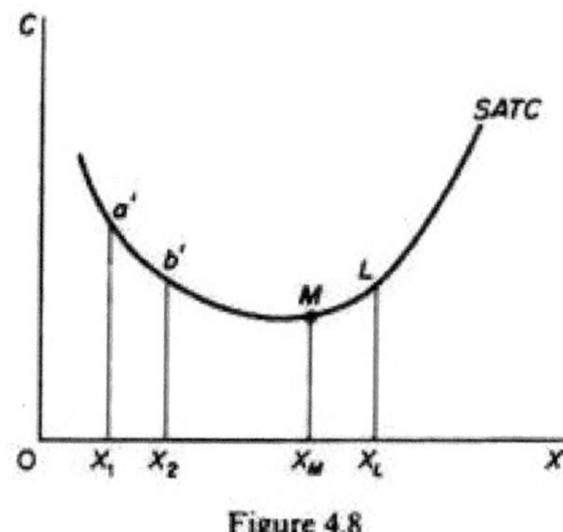

Figure 4.8

The U shape of both the AVC and the ATC reflects the law of variable proportions or law of eventually decreasing returns to the variable factor(s) of production. The marginal cost is defined as the change in TC which results from a unit change in output. Mathematically the marginal cost is the first derivative of the TC function. Denoting total cost by C and output by X we have

$MC = \partial C / \partial X$

Graphically the MC is the slope of the TC curve (which of course is the same at any point as the slope of the TVC). The slope of a curve at any one of its points is the slope of the tangent at that point. With an inverse-S shape of the TC (and TVC) the MC curve will be U-shaped. In figure 4.9 we observe that the slope of the tangent to the total-cost curve declines gradually, until it becomes parallel to the X-axis (with its slope being equal to zero at this point), and then starts rising. Accordingly, we picture the MC curve in figure 4.10 as U-shaped.

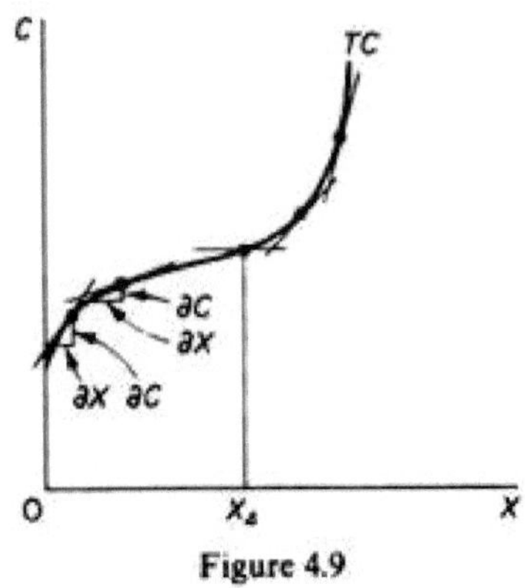

Figure 4.9

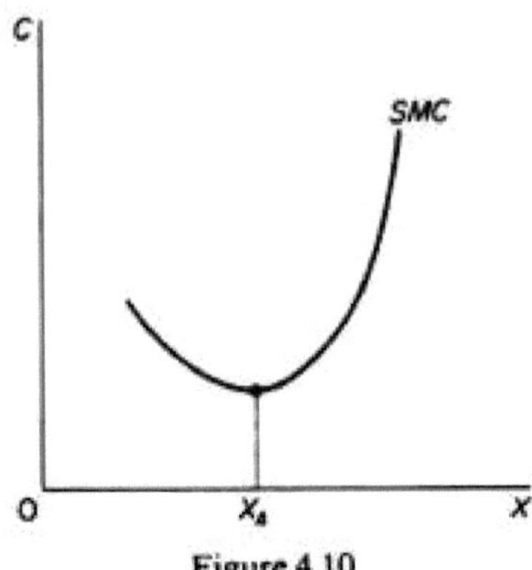

Figure 4.10

In summary: the traditional theory of costs postulates that in the short run the cost curves (AVC, ATC and MC) is U-shaped, reflecting the law of variable proportions. In the short run with a fixed plant there is a phase of increasing productivity (falling unit costs) and a phase of decreasing productivity (increasing unit costs) of the variable factor(s).

Between these two phases of plant operation there is a single point at which unit costs are at a minimum. When this point on the SATC is reached the plant is utilized optimally, that is, with the optimal combination (proportions) of fixed and variable factors.

The relationship between ATC and AVC:

The AVC is a part of the ATC, given ATC = AFC + AVC. Both AVC and ATC are U-shaped, reflecting the law of variable proportions. However, the minimum point of the ATC occurs to the right of the minimum point of the AVC (figure 4.11). This is due to the fact that ATC includes AFC, and the latter falls continuously with increases in output.

After the AVC has reached its lowest point and starts rising, its rise is over a certain range offset by the fall in the AFC, so that the ATC continues to fall (over that range) despite the increase in AVC. However, the rise in AVC eventually becomes greater than the fall in the AFC so that the A TC starts increasing. The A VC approaches the A TC asymptotically as X increases.

In figure 4.11 the minimum AVC is reached at X_1 while the ATC is at its minimum at X_2. Between X_1 and X_2 the fall in AFC more than offsets the rise in AVC so that the ATC continues to fall. Beyond X_2 the increase in AVC is not offset by the fall in AFC so that ATC rises.

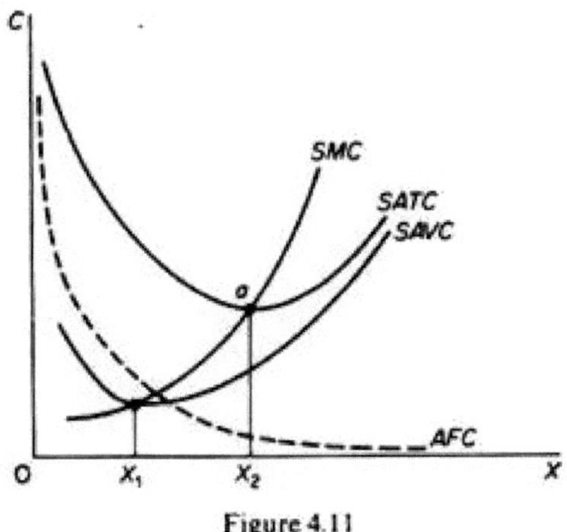

Figure 4.11

The relationship between MC and ATC:

The MC cuts the ATC and the AVC at their lowest points. We will establish this relation only for the ATC and MC, but the relationship between MC and AVC can be established on the same lines of reasoning.

We said that the MC is the change in the TC for producing an extra unit of output. Assume that we start from a level of n units of output. If we increase the output by one unit the MC is the change in total cost resulting from the production of the $(n + 1)^{th}$ unit.

The AC at each level of output is found by dividing TC by X. Thus the AC at the level of X_n is

$$AC_n = \frac{TC_n}{X_n}$$

and the AC at the level X_{n+1} is

$$AC_{n+1} = \frac{TC_{n+1}}{X_{n+1}}$$

Clearly

$$TC_{n+1} = TC_n + MC$$

Thus:

(a) If the MC of the $(n + 1)^{th}$ unit is less than AC_n (the AC of the previous n units) the AC_{n+1} will be smaller than the AC_n.

(b) If the MC of the $(n + 1)^{th}$ unit is higher than AC_n (the AC of the previous n units) the AC_{n+1} will be higher than the AC_n.

So long as the MC lies below the AC curve, it pulls the latter downwards; when the MC rises above the AC, it pulls the latter upwards. In figure 4.11 to the left of an MC lies below the AC curve, and hence the latter falls downwards. To the right of an MC, the curve lies above the AC curve so that AC rises. It follows that at point a, where the intersection of the MC and AC occurs, the AC has reached its minimum level.

B. Long-Run Costs of the Traditional Theory: The 'Envelope' Curve:

In the long run, all factors are assumed to become variable. We said that the long-run cost curve is a planning curve, in the sense that it is a guide to the entrepreneur in his decision to plan the future expansion of his output. The long-run average-cost curve is derived from short-run cost curves. Each point on the LAC corresponds to a point on a short-run cost curve, which is tangent to the LAC at that point. Let us examine in detail how the LAC is derived from the SRC curves.

Assume, as a first approximation, that the available technology to the firm at a particular point of time includes three methods of production, each with a different plant size: a small plant, medium plant and large plant. The small plant operates with costs denoted by the curve SAC_1, the medium-size plant operates with the costs on SAC_2 and the large-size plant gives rise to the costs shown on SAC_3 (figure 4.12). If the firm plans to produce output X_3 it will choose the small plant. If it plans to produce X_2 it will choose the medium plant. If it wishes to produce X_1 it will choose the large-size plant.

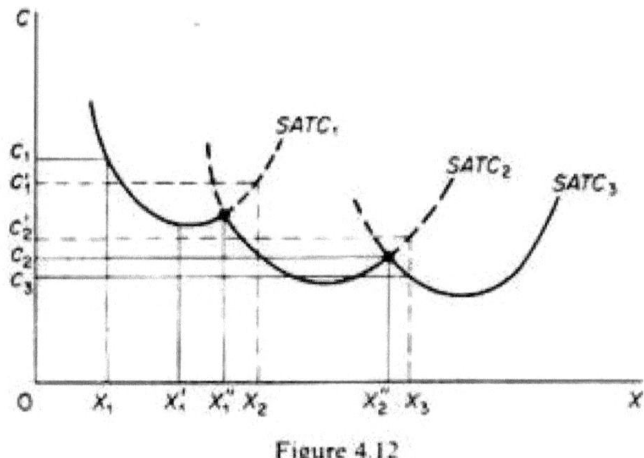

Figure 4.12

If the firm starts with the small plant and its demand gradually increases, it will produce at lower costs (up to level X'_1). Beyond that point, costs start increasing. If its demand reaches the level X''_1 the firm can either continue to produce with the small plant or it can install the medium-size plant. The decision at this point depends not on costs but on the firm's expectations about its future demand. If the firm expects that the demand will expand further than X''_1 it will install the medium plant, because with this plant outputs larger than X'_1 are produced with a lower cost.

Similar considerations hold for the decision of the firm when it reaches the level X''_2. If it expects its demand to stay constant at this level, the firm will not install the large plant, given that it involves a larger investment which is profitable only if demand expands beyond X''_2. For example, the level of output X_3 is produced at a cost c_3 with the large plant, while it costs c'_2 if produced with the medium-size plant ($c'_2 > c_3$).

Now if we relax the assumption of the existence of only three plants and assume that the available technology includes many plant sizes, each suitable for a certain level of output, the points of intersection of consecutive plants (which are the crucial points for the decision of whether to switch to a larger plant) are more numerous. In the limit, if we assume that there is a very large number (infinite number) of plants, we obtain a continuous curve, which is the planning LAC curve of the firm.

Each point of this curve shows the minimum (optimal) cost for producing the corresponding level of output. The LAC curve is the locus of points denoting the least cost of producing the corresponding output. It is a planning curve because on the basis of this curve the firm decides what plant to set up in order to produce optimally (at minimum cost) the expected level of output.

The firm chooses the short-run plant which allows it to produce the anticipated (in the long run) output at the least possible cost. In the traditional theory of the firm, the LAC curve is U-shaped and it is often called the 'envelope curve' because it 'envelopes' the SRC curves (figure 4.13).

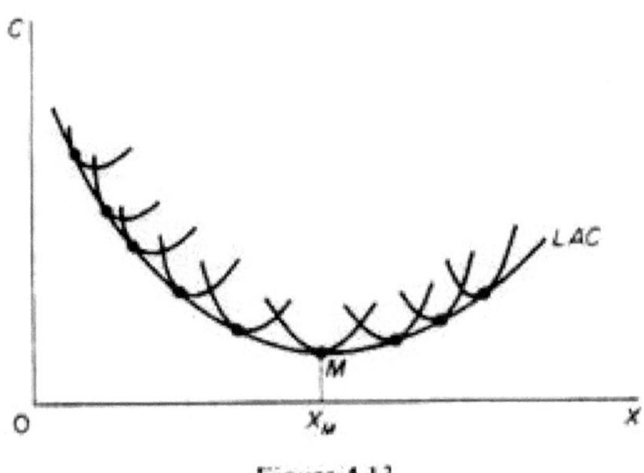

Figure 4.13

Let us examine the U shape of the LAC. This shape reflects the laws of returns to scale. According to these laws the unit costs of production decrease as plant size increases, due to the economies of scale that the larger plant sizes make possible. The traditional theory of the firm assumes that economies of scale exist only up to a certain size of the plant, which is known as the optimum plant size because with this plant size all possible economies of scale are fully exploited.

If the plant increases further than this optimum size there are diseconomies of scale, arising from managerial inefficiencies. It is argued that management becomes highly complex, managers are overworked and the decision-making process becomes less efficient. The turning-up of the LAC curve is due to managerial diseconomies of scale since the technical diseconomies can be avoided by duplicating the optimum technical plant size.

A serious implicit assumption of the traditional U-shaped cost curves is that each plant size is designed to produce optimally a single level of output (e.g. 1000 units of X). Any departure from that X, no matter how small (e.g. an increase by 1 unit of X) leads to increased costs. The plant is completely inflexible. There is no reserve capacity, not even to meet seasonal variations in demand.

As a consequence of this assumption the LAC curve 'envelopes' the SRAC. Each point of the LAC is a point of tangency with the corresponding SRAC curve. The point of tangency occurs to the falling part of the SRAC curves for points lying to the left of the minimum point of the LAC since the slope of the LAC is negative up to M (figure 4.13) the slope of the SRMC curves must also be negative, since at the point of their tangency the two curves have the same slope.

The point of tangency for outputs larger than X_M occurs to the rising part of the SRAC curves since the LAC rises, the SAC must rise at the point of their tangency with the LAC. Only at the minimum point M of the LAC is the corresponding SAC also at a minimum. Thus at the falling part of the LAC the plants are not worked to full capacity; to the rising part of the LAC the plants are overworked; only at the minimum point M is the (short-run) plant optimally employed.

We stress once more the optimality implied by the LAC planning curve each point represents the least unit-cost for producing the corresponding level of output. Any point above the LAC is inefficient in that it shows a higher cost for producing the corresponding level of output. Any point below the LAC is economically desirable because it implies a lower unit cost, but it is not attainable in the current state of technology and with the prevailing market prices of factors of production. (Recall that each cost curve is drawn under a ceteris paribus clause, which implies given state of technology and given factor prices.)

The long-run marginal cost is derived from the SRMC curves but does not 'envelope' them. The LRMC is formed from points of intersection of the SRMC curves with vertical lines (to the X-axis) drawn from the points of tangency of the corresponding SAC curves and the LRA cost curve (figure

4.14). The LMC must be equal to the SMC for the output at which the corresponding SAC is tangent to the LAC. For levels of X to the left of tangency a the SAC > LAC

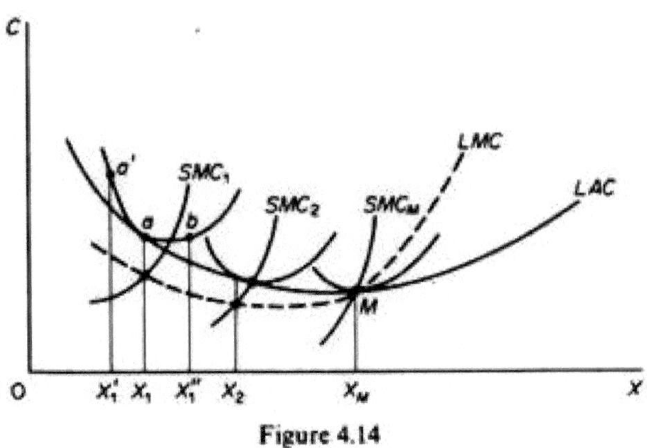

Figure 4.14

At the point of tangency SAC = LAC. As we move from point a' to a, we actually move from a position of inequality of SRAC and LRAC to a position of equality. Hence the change in total cost (i.e. the MC) must be smaller for the short-run curve than for the long-run curve. Thus LMC > SMC to the left of a. For an increase in output beyond X, (e.g. X'_1) the SAC > LAC. That is, we move from the position a of equality of the two costs to the position b where SAC is greater than LAC. Hence the addition to total cost (= MC) must be larger for the short-run curve than for the long-run curve. Thus LMC < SMC to the right of a.

Since to the left of a, LMC > SMC, and to the right of a, LMC < SMC, it follows that at a, LMC – SMC. If we draw a vertical line from a to the X-axis the point at which it intersects the SMC (point A for SAC_1) is a point of the LMC.

If we repeat this procedure for all points of tangency of SRAC and LAC curves to the left of the minimum point of the LAC, we obtain points of the section of the LMC which lies below the LAC. At the minimum point M, the LMC intersects the LAC. To the right of M the LMC lies above the LAC curve. At point M we have

$SAC_M = SMC_M = LAC = LMC$

There are various mathematical forms which give rise to U-shaped unit cost curves. The simplest total cost function which would incorporate the law of variable proportions is the cubic polynomial

The TC curve is roughly S-shaped, while the ATC, the AVC, and the MC are all U-shaped; the MC curve intersects the other two curves at their minimum points (figure 4.11).

Modern Theory Of Cost

Modern economists including **Stigler, Andrews, and Friedman** have questioned the validity of U-shaped cost curves both theoretical as well as on empirical grounds. Also the long-run costs in modern theory are not U-shaped but L- shaped.

The Modern theory suggests the existence of 'built- in- reserve capacity 'which imparts flexibility and enables the plant to produce larger output without adding to the costs. Built –in- reserve capacities are planned by firms.

The short-run cost curve has a saucer- type shape whereas the long-run Average cost curve is either L-Shaped or inverse J-shaped.

The Modern theory of cost stresses the role of economies of scale, which significantly enables the firm to continue production at the lowest point of average cost for a considerable period of time. The firm checks dis-economies of scale by planning in advance and enjoys the gains of production in comparison to the traditional theory where the average cost rises after the firm reaches the optimal level of output.

Types Of Costs As Per Modern Theory Of Cost

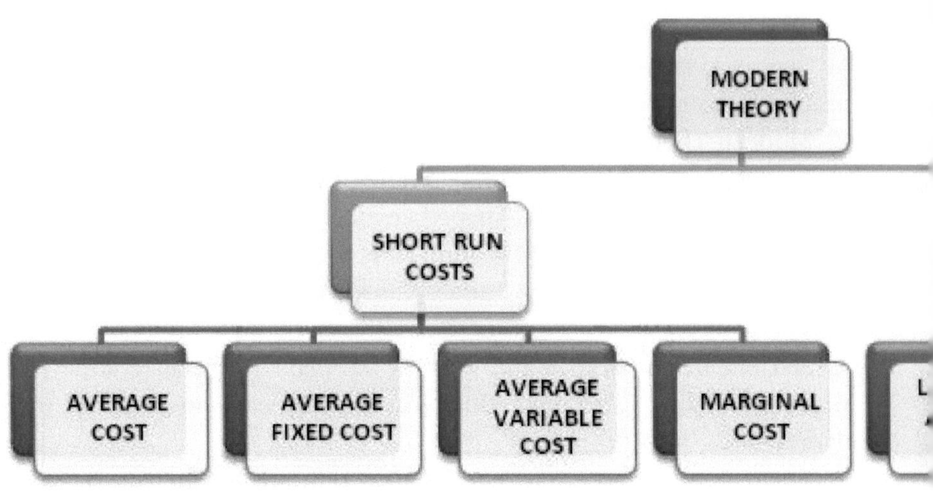

Modern Theory Of Cost-Short Run Costs

Average Fixed Cost

The fixed costs include the costs for:

- The salaries and other expenses of administrative staff.
- The wear and tear of machinery.
- The expenses for maintenance of building.
- The expenses for the maintenance of land on which the plant is installed or operates.

As in the traditional theory of cost, the average fixed costs in modern microeconomics, also plots as a rectangular hyperbola. This is shown as follows:

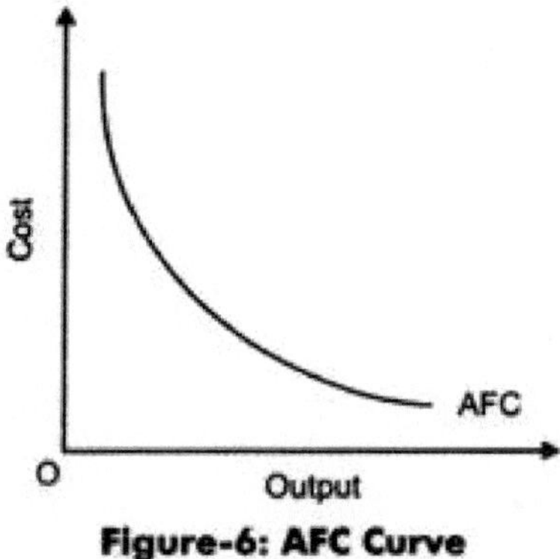

Figure-6: AFC Curve

Modern Theory of Cost

Average Vvariable Cost

In modern theory, Average variable cost is not U shaped rather it is saucer shaped and has a flat stretch over a range of output. This flat stretch represents the 'built in reserve capacity' of the firm to meet seasonal and cyclical changes in the demand. The average variable cost curve is as follows:

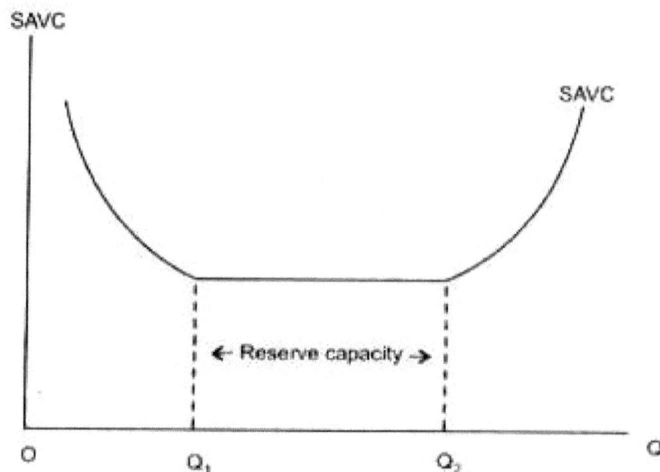

Average Cost

The short-run Average costs consist of the Average fixed costs and Average variable costs. The short-run average variable cost curve at each level of output. The smooth and continuous fall in the average cost curve is due to the fact that the AFC curve is a rectangular hyperbola and the AVC curve first falls and then becomes horizontal within the range of reserve capacity. Beyond that it starts rising steeply. The curve of average cost is as follows:

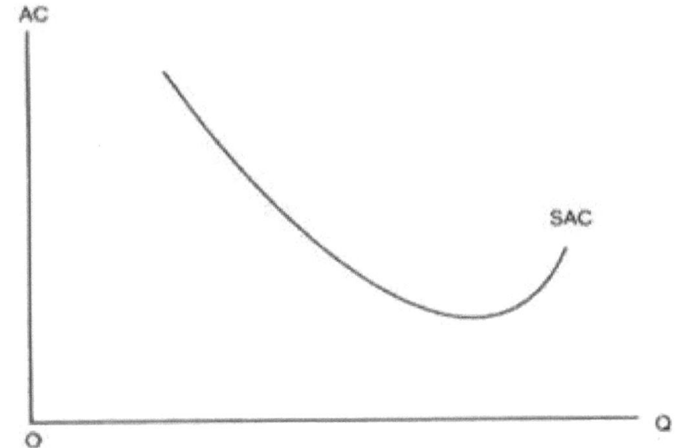

Fig. 5.13: *The short run AC in the modern theory of costs.*

Modern Theory Of Cost-Long Run Costs

Long Run Average Cost

Modern economists divide long run costs into production costs and managerial costs/ In the long run, all costs are variable and they given rise to a long run average cost curve which is roughly L- shaped. This curve rapidly slopes downwards in the beginning but later remains flat or slopes gently downwards at its right-hand cost. The long run average cost curve is as follows:

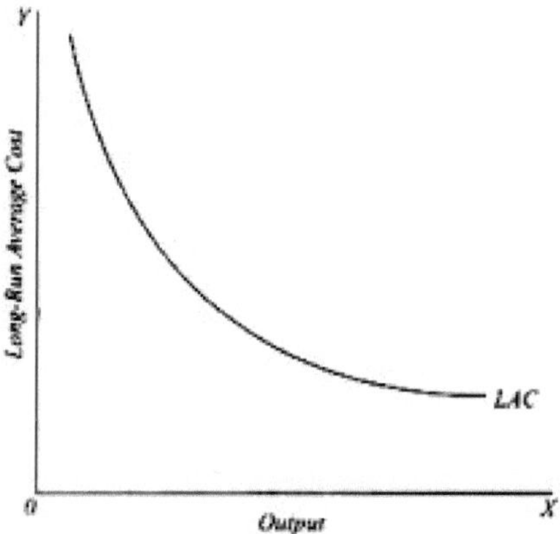

Fig. 19.17. L-Shaped Long-Rum Average Cost Curve

Long Run Marginal Cost

The Long run average costs curve has two main features:

- It does not rise at every large scale of output.
- It does not envelope the Short run Average Cost but intersects them

According to modern theory, shape of long-run marginal cost curve corresponds to the shape of long-run average cost curve. The given figure shows that when LAC is L- shaped and LAC curve is falling then LMC curve will also be falling and its falling portion will be below the falling portion of LAC curve.

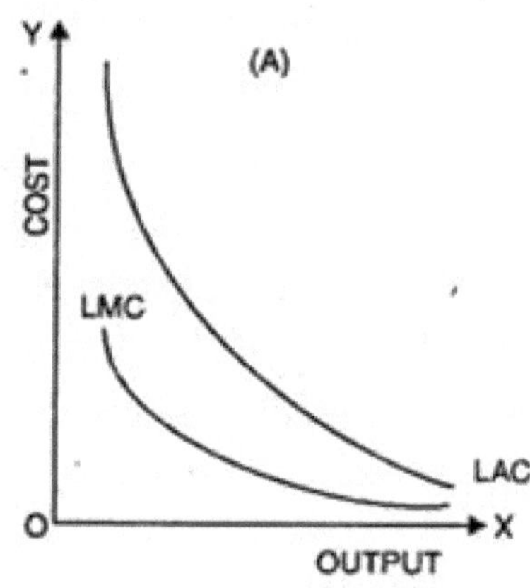

Long run marginal cost is defined at the additional cost of producing an extra unit of the output in the long-run i.e. when all inputs are variable. The LMC curve is derived by the points of tangency between LAC and SAC.

Note an important relation between LMC and SAC here. When LMC lies below LAC, LAC is falling, while when LMC is above LAC, LAC is rising. At the point where LMC = LAC, LAC is constant and minimum.

Solved Example for You

Question: Why is the LAC also called the envelope curve?

Answer: The LAC curve suggests the long run optimization problem of the firm. The firm can choose a plant size to operate at in the long-run where all inputs are variable. Thus, the firm shall choose that plant at which it can minimize costs.

So, the LAC is derived by joining the minimum most points of all possible SAC curves of the firm at different output levels. Since the LAC thus obtained almost 'envelopes' the SAC curves faced by the firm, it is called the envelope curve.

- **Economies of Scale**

Economies of Scale the economies of scale determine the shape of the long-run average cost curve. As the size of the plant and the scale of operation become larger, certain economies of scale are usually realised. Factors like specialisation and division of labour and other technological improvements enable producers to reduce the unit cost. These factors give rise to a negatively sloped position of the LRAC. The rising portion of the LAC is usually attributed to the "diseconomies of scale". Such a feature could take place due to limitations in efficient management. It is difficult to determine just when diseconomies of scale set in and when they become strong enough to outweigh the economies of scale. In 46 Producer Behaviour businesses where economies scale are negligible, diseconomies may soon become of paramount importance and cause the LAC to turn up at a relatively small volume of output. Panel A of Figure 5.16 shows the LRAC for such a firm. Sometimes the LAC may not turn upward until a very large volume of output is attained. This is shown in panel B of Figure 5.16. It is the case of 'natural monopolies'. In many situations, a very modest scale of operation may enable firm to capture all the economies of scale. Diseconomies may not be incurred until the volume of output is very high.

In such a case, LAC would have a horizontal stretch, as shown in panel (C). O LAC C Panel A O LAC C Panel B O LAC C Panel C

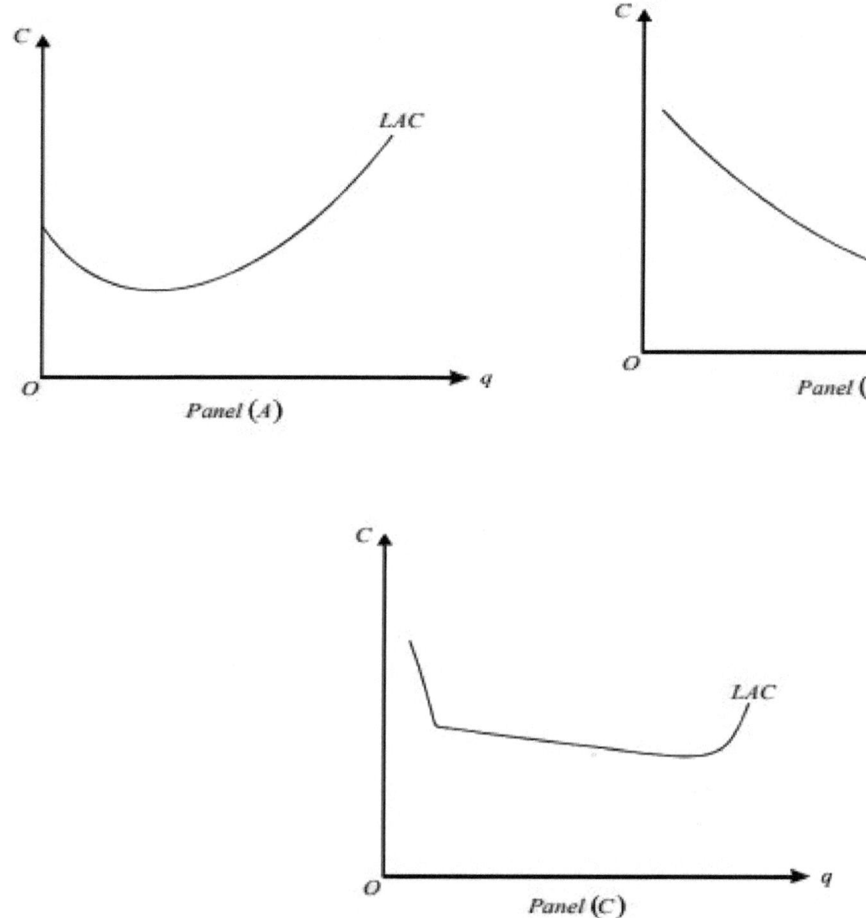

Different Types of LAC
Types of Economies of Scale

1. **Internal Economies of Scale**

This refers to economies that are unique to a firm. For instance, a firm may hold a patent over a mass production machine, which allows it to lower its average cost of production more than other firms in the industry.

1. **External Economies of Scale**

These refer to economies of scale enjoyed by an entire industry. For instance, suppose the government wants to increase steel production. In order to do so, the government announces that all steel producers who employ more than 10,000 workers will be given a 20% tax break.

Thus, firms employing less than 10,000 workers can potentially lower their average cost of production by employing more workers. This is an example of an external economy of scale – one that affects an entire industry or sector of the economy.

Sources of Economies of Scale

- Purchasing Firms might be able to lower average costs by buying the inputs required for the production process in bulk or from special wholesalers.
- Managerial Firms might be able to lower average costs by improving the management structure within the firm. The firm might hire better skilled or more experienced managers.

Technological .A technological advancement might drastically change the production process. For instance, fracking completely changed the oil industry a few years ago.

However, only large oil firms that could afford to invest in expensive fracking equipment could take advantage of the new technology. Diseconomies of Scale consider the graph shown above. Any increase in output beyond Q2 leads to a rise in average costs. This is an example of diseconomies of scale – a rise in average costs due to an increase in the scale of production. As firms get larger, they grow in complexity. Such firms need to balance the economies of scale against the diseconomies of scale. For instance, a firm might be able to implement certain economies of scale in its marketing division if it increased output. However, increasing output might result in diseconomies of scale in the firm"s management division.

Frederick Herzberg, a distinguished professor of management, suggested a reason why companies should not blindly target economies of scale: ***"Numbers numb our feelings for what is being counted and lead to adoration of the economies of scale. Passion is in feeling the quality of experience, not in trying to measure it."***

- **Economies of Scope**

What is Economies of Scope?

Economies of degree is a financial idea that the unit cost to deliver an item will decrease as the assortment of items increments. That is, the more unique yet comparative merchandise you produce, the lower the all-out cost to deliver every one.

For instance, suppose that you're a shoe maker. You produce people's tennis shoes. Adding a youngsters' line of shoes would build economies of degree since you can utilize similar creation hardware, supplies, stockpiling, and appropriation channels to make another line of items. That will additionally diminish the expense of creation on the entirety of your shoes.

The expense to deliver every one of the three of your various lines is lower than if three distinct organizations each created a line of men's shoes, a line of ladies' shoes, and a youngsters' line. Since you can expand the utilization of your assets to make more items to be offered to your equivalent objective market, you can keep on driving expenses down.

Key Points

- Producing two or more products at the same time at a lower cost than producing them separately is referred to as economies of scope.
- Instead of focusing on one product at a time, a company might use similar raw materials and production units to produce a variety of products.
- It's a fantastic concept that can be realised through various strategies such as flexible manufacturing, product diversification, supply chain linking, and mergers and acquisitions.
- The concept has exploded in popularity, with applications in manufacturing, operations, banking, and IT services.

Examples of Economies of Scope

- Many industries are looking into ways to improve their businesses by utilising economies of scale, which we will demonstrate with an example.
- Aside from e-commerce, the banking industry also benefits from economies of scale. Traditional banking, investment banking, credit card services, trading services, wealth management, and mutual fund services

are all offered by banks with a strong IT infrastructure.

- After establishing the IT infrastructure, tech-savvy banks were able to provide a wide range of services without incurring the additional costs that would have resulted from arranging additional units for each service.

Market Structures

What is Market Structure?

Market structure, in financial matters, alludes to how various enterprises are characterized and separated in view of their certification and nature of rivalry for labor and products. It depends on the attributes that impact the conduct and results of organizations working in a particular market.

Market Structure

A portion of the elements that decide a market structure incorporate the quantity of purchasers and venders, capacity to arrange, level of focus, level of separation of items, and the simplicity or trouble of entering and leaving the market.

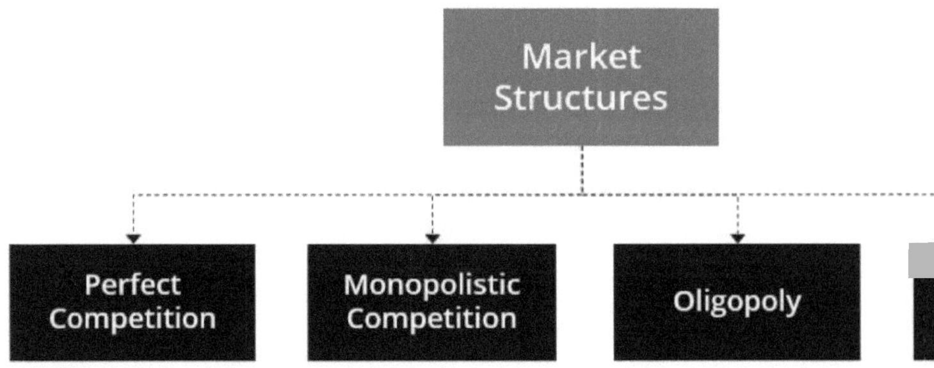

Source:corporatefinanceinstitute.com

Key Points

- Market structure alludes to how various enterprises are ordered and separated in light of their certificate and nature of rivalry for administrations and merchandise.
- The four famous sorts of market structures incorporate amazing rivalry, oligopoly market, restraining infrastructure market, and monopolistic contest.

- Market structures show the relations among venders and different merchants, dealers to purchasers, or more.

Understanding Market Structures

In financial aspects, market designs can be seen well by intently inspecting a variety of variables or elements displayed by various players. It is normal to separate these business sectors across the accompanying seven unmistakable highlights.

- The business' purchaser structure
- The turnover of clients
- The degree of item separation
- The idea of expenses of data sources
- The quantity of players on the lookout
- Vertical incorporation degree in a similar industry
- The biggest player's portion of the overall industry

By interviewing the above highlights against one another, comparable characteristics can be laid out. Accordingly, it becomes simpler to arrange and separate organizations across related ventures. In view of the above highlights, financial analysts have utilized this data to portray four particular sorts of market structures. They incorporate amazing rivalry, oligopoly market, restraining infrastructure market, and monopolistic contest.

When the competition is high there is a high supply of commodity as different companies try to dominate the markets and it also creates barriers to entry for the companies that intend to join that market. A monopoly market has the biggest level of barriers to entry while the perfectly competitive market has zero percent level of barriers to entry. Firms are more efficient in a competitive market than in a monopoly structure.

The Perfect Competition

Perfect competition exists when buyers and sellers are so numerous and well-informed in a market that all elements of monopoly are absent, and the market price of a commodity is beyond the control of individual buyers and sellers.

When there are many firms and a homogeneous product, no single firm can influence the price of the product, implying that the price elasticity of demand for a single firm will be infinite.

Monopolistic Competition

Monopolistic rivalry is a type of market structure in which countless free firms are providing items that are somewhat separated according to the perspective of purchasers. In this manner, the results of the contending firms are close however flawed substitutes since purchasers don't see them as indistinguishable. The present circumstance emerges when a similar item is being sold under various brand names, each brand being marginally not quite the same as the others.

Monopoly

Monopoly is said to exist when one firm is the sole maker or vender of an item which has no nearby substitutes. As per this definition, there should be a solitary maker or dealer of an item. Assuming there are numerous makers delivering an item, either amazing contest or monopolistic rivalry will win contingent on whether the item is homogeneous or separated.

- From above it follows that for the syndication to exist, following things are fundamental.
- One and only one firm delivers and sells a specific ware or a help.
- There are no adversaries or direct contenders of the firm.
- No other merchant can enter the market for whatever reasons legitimate, specialized, or monetary.

Monopolist is a value creator. He attempts to take the best of anything request and cost conditions exist without the apprehension about new firms entering to contend away his benefits.

Oligopoly

In an oligopolistic market there are modest number of firms so venders are aware of their relationship. The opposition is more than a little flawed, yet the competition among firms is high. Considering that there are huge number of potential responses of contenders, the conduct of firms might accept different structures. Accordingly there are different models of oligopolistic conduct, each in view of various responses examples of adversaries.

Oligopoly is what is happening in which a couple of firms are contending on the lookout for a specific item. The separating attributes of oligopoly are with the end goal that neither the hypothesis of monopolistic contest nor the hypothesis of restraining infrastructure can clarify the conduct of an oligopolistic firm.For Example – Aircraft producing, in certain nations:

remote correspondence, media, and banking.

- **Price-Output decisions under Perfect Competition**

Perfect competition refers to a market situation where there are a large number of buyers and sellers dealing in homogenous products.

Moreover, under perfect competition, there are no legal, social, or technological barriers on the entry or exit of organizations. In perfect competition, sellers and buyers are fully aware about the current market price of a product. Therefore, none of them sell or buy at a higher rate. As a result, the same price prevails in the market under perfect competition.

Under perfect competition, the buyers and sellers cannot influence the market price by increasing or decreasing their purchases or output, respectively. The market price of products in perfect competition is determined by the industry. This implies that in perfect competition, the market price of products is determined by taking into account two market forces, namely market demand and market supply.

In the words of Marshall, "Both the elements of demand and supply are required for the determination of price of a commodity in the same manner as both the blades of scissors are required to cut a cloth." As discussed in the previous chapters, market demand is defined as a sum of the quantity demanded by each individual organizations in the industry.

On the other hand, market supply refers to the sum of the quantity supplied by individual organizations in the industry. In perfect competition, the price of a product is determined at a point at which the demand and supply curve intersect each other. This point is known as equilibrium point as well as the price is known as equilibrium price. In addition, at this point, the quantity demanded and supplied is called equilibrium quantity. Let us discuss price determination under perfect competition in the next sections.

Demand under Perfect Competition:

Demand refers to the quantity of a product that consumers are willing to purchase at a particular price, while other factors remain constant. A consumer demands more quantity at lower price and less quantity at higher price. Therefore, the demand varies at different prices.

Figure-1 represents the demand curve under perfect competition:

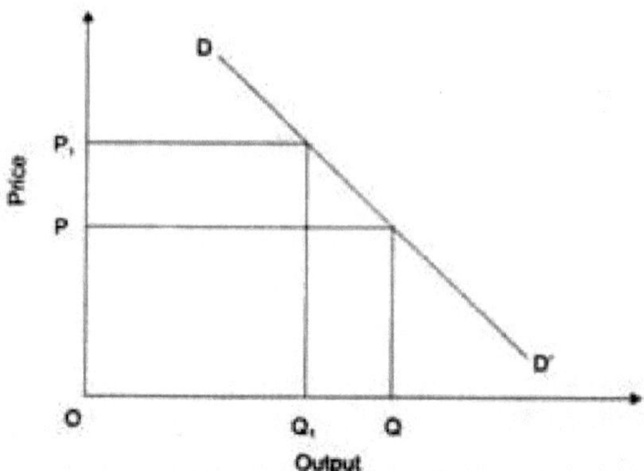

Figure-1: Demand Curve under Perfect Competition

As shown in Figure-1, when price is OP, the quantity demanded is OQ. On the other hand, when price increases to OP1, the quantity demanded reduces to OQ1. Therefore, under perfect competition, the demand curve (DD'') slopes downward. Supply under Perfect Competition: Supply refers to quantity of a product that producers are willing to supply at a particular price. Generally, the supply of a product increases at high price and decreases at low price.

Figure-2 shows the supply curve under perfect competition:

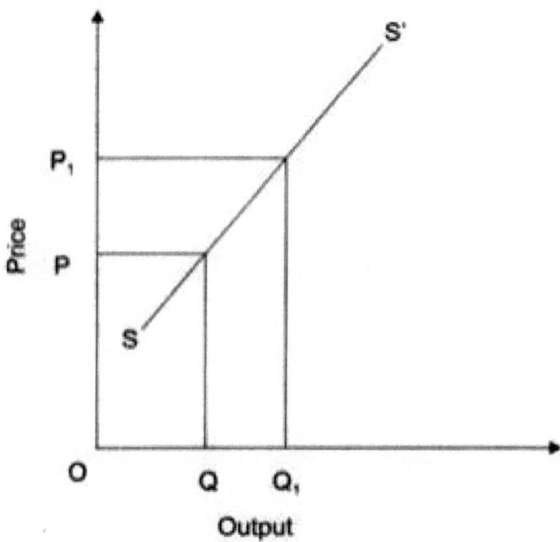

Figure-2: Supply Curve under Perfect Competition

In Figure-2, the quantity supplied is OQ at price OP. When price increases to OP1, the quantity supplied increases to OQ1. This is because the producers are able to earn large profits by supplying products at higher price. Therefore, under perfect competition, the supply curves (SS") slopes upward.

Equilibrium under Perfect Competition:

As discussed earlier, in perfect competition, the price of a product is determined at a point at which the demand and supply curve intersect each other. This point is known as equilibrium point. At this point, the quantity demanded and supplied is called equilibrium quantity.

Figure-3 shows the equilibrium under perfect competition:

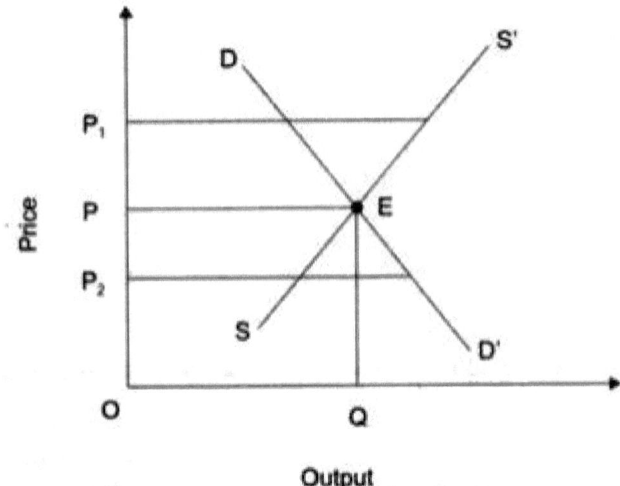

Figure-3: Price and Output Determination under Perfect Competition

In Figure-3, it can be seen that at price OP1, supply is more than the demand. Therefore, prices will fall down to OP. Similarly, at price OP2, demand is more than the supply. Similarly, in such a case, the prices will rise to OP. Thus, E is the equilibrium at which equilibrium price is OP and equilibrium quantity is OQ.

Supply Curve Of The Firm And Industry Under Perfect Competition

Supply Curve of a Firm and Industry: Short-Run and Long-Run Supply Curve!

Supply curve indicates the relationship between price and quantity supplied. In other words, supply curve shows the quantities that a seller is willing to sell at different prices.

According to Dorfman, "Supply curve is that curve which indicates various quantities supplied by the firm at different prices". The concept of supply curve applies only under the conditions of perfect competition.

Supply curve can be divided into two parts as:

A. Short Run Supply Curve

B. Long Run Supply Curve A.

Short Run Supply Curve

i. Short Run Supply Curve of a Firm:

Short run is a period in which supply can be changed by changing only the variable factors, fixed factors remaining the same. That way, if the firm shuts down, it has to bear fixed costs. That is why in the short run, the firm will supply commodity till price is either greater or equal to average variable cost. Thus a firm will continue supplying the commodity till marginal cost is equal to price or average revenue. Under perfect competition average revenue is equal to marginal revenue, so the firm will produce up to that point where marginal revenue and marginal cost are equal.

Short run supply curve of a perfectly competitive firm is that portion of marginal cost curve which is above average variable cost curve. According to C.E. Ferguson, "The short run supply curve of a firm in perfect competition is precisely its Marginal Cost Curve for all rates of output equal to or greater than the rate of output associated with minimum average variable cost." Prof. Bilas has defined it in simple words, "The Firm"s short period supply curve is that portion of its marginal cost curve that lies-above the minimum point of the average variable cost curve." However, short run supply curve of a firm can be shown with the help of fig. 1.

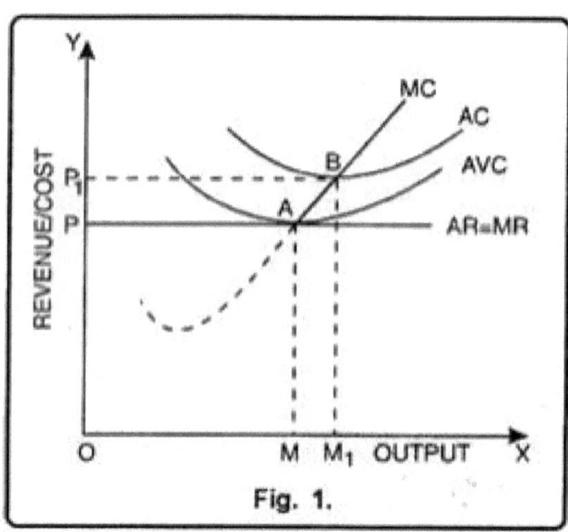

Fig. 1.

From fig. 1 it is clear that there is no supply if price is below OP. At price less than OP, the firm will not be covering its average variable cost. At OP price, OM is the supply. In this case, firms" marginal revenue and marginal cost cut each other at A, OM is equilibrium output. If price goes up to OP1, the firm will produce OM1 output. This firm"s short run supply curve starts from A upwards i.e., thick line AB.

ii. Short Run Supply Curve of an Industry: An industry is a blend of firms producing homogeneous goods. That way, supply curve of an industry is a lateral summation of all firms. This can be made clear with the help of a Fig. 2.

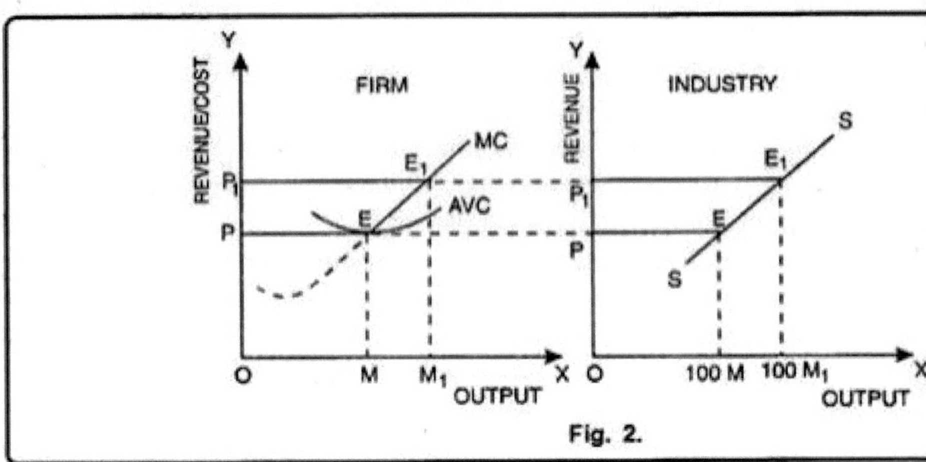

Fig. 2.

Here, we have assumed that different firms in the industry are producing identical products.

Each firm at OP price is producing OM output. It is because all firms have identical costs. At OP price, supply of industry is 100 x M = 100M.

Similarly at OP1 price, all the firms of industry are producing 100 xM1 =100M1 quantity of output. These quantities will be called supply or output of industry. SS is the supply curve of industry. Point E shows that at OP price firm"s supply is OM and an industry"s total supply is 100 × M = 100M.

At OP1 price, firm"s supply is OM1 and industry"s supply is 100M). We get industry"s supply curve by joining points E and E1.

Thus, under perfect competition, lateral summation of that part of short run marginal cost curves of the firms which lie above the average variable cost constitutes the supply curve of the industry. According to Stonier and Hague, "short run supply curve of a competitive industry will always slope upwards since the short run marginal cost curve of the industrial firms always slope upward."

B. Long Run Supply Curve:

Long run supply curve can also be analyzed from firm and industry's point of view: 1. Long Run Supply Curve of a Firm:

Long run is a period in which supply can be changed by changing all the factors of production. There is no distinction between fixed and variable factors. In the long run, firm produces only at minimum average cost. In this situation, long run marginal cost, marginal revenue, average revenue and long run average cost are equal i.e., LMCMR (= AR)LAC (minimum). The firm is enjoying only normal profits.

So that position of marginal cost curve will determine the supply curve which is above the minimum average variable cost. The point where minimum average cost is equal to marginal cost is called optimum production. Thus Long Run Supply Curve of a firm is that portion of its marginal cost curve that lies above the minimum point of the average cost curve.

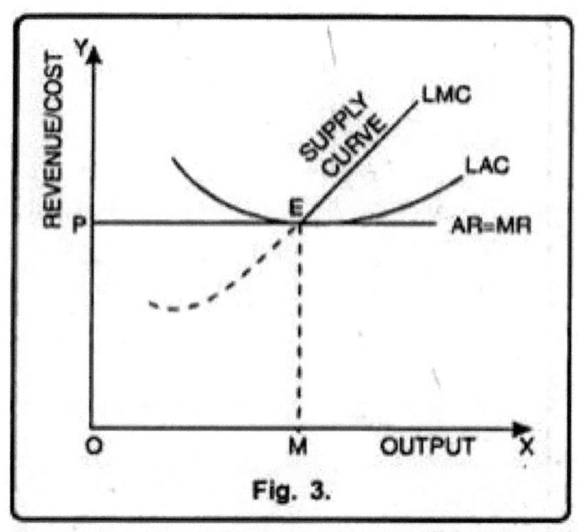

Fig. 3.

In figure 3 the firm is in equilibrium at point E where MRLMC (=AR). AC is minimum corresponding to this point. This point E is also called optimum point because at this point MR=LMCAR minimum LAC. That portion of LMC which is above E is called long run supply curve.

2. Long Run Supply Curve of an Industry:

In the long run, industry"s supply curve is determined by the supply curve of firms in the long run. Long run supply curve in the long run is not lateral summation of the short run supply curves. Industry"s long run supply curve depends upon the change in the optimum size of firms and change in the number of firms.

It is on account of two reasons:

i. In the long run, firms continue to enter into and exit from the industry,
ii. Firms get economies and diseconomies of scale. This displaces the long run marginal cost (LMC).

Due to these reasons, long run supply curve of industry is not the lateral summation of supply curve of firms. In reality, long run supply curve of industry can be known from the long run optimum production of firms multiplied by the number of firms in an industry.

LRSi , = Q x N

Where LRS1 is long run supply curve of industry. Q is the optimum output of a firm and N, the number of firms.

- **Monopoly**

Meaning:

The word monopoly has been derived from the combination of two words i.e., 'Mono' and 'Poly'. Mono refers to a single and poly to control.

In this way, monopoly refers to a market situation in which there is only one seller of a commodity.

Definition:

Monopoly is a situation where there is a single seller in the market.

In conventional economic analysis, the monopoly case is taken as the polar opposite of perfect competition. By definition, the demand curve facing the monopolist is the industry demand curve which is downward sloping. Thus, the monopolist has significant power over the price it charges, i.e. is a price setter rather than a price taker.

In a monopoly market, factors like government license, ownership of resources, copyright and patent and high starting cost make an entity a single seller of goods. All these factors restrict the entry of other sellers in the market. Monopolies also possess some information that is not known to other sellers.

Characteristics associated with a monopoly market make the single seller the market controller as well as the price maker. He enjoys the power of setting the price for his goods.

"Pure monopoly is represented by a market situation in which there is a single seller of a product for which there are no substitutes; this single seller is unaffected by and does not affect the prices and outputs of other products sold in the economy." **Bilas**

"A pure monopoly exists when there is only one producer in the market. There are no dire competitions." –**Ferguson**

Comparison of monopoly and perfectly competitive outcomes reveals that the monopolist will set a higher price, produce a lower output and earn above normal profits (sometimes referred to as monopoly rents). This suggests that consumers will face a higher price, leading to a deadweight welfare loss. In addition, income will be transferred from consumers to the monopoly firm.

Monopoly should be distinguished from market power. The latter is a term which refers to all situations in which firms face downward sloping demand curves and can profitably raise price above the competitive level. Market power may arise not only when there is a monopoly, but also when there is oligopoly, monopolistic competition, or a dominant firm.

Features of a Monopoly

After monopoly definition, let's take a look at the features of a monopoly:

1. **Single seller and several buyers**

The primary feature of a monopoly is a single seller and several buyers. Also, in a monopoly, there is no difference between the firm and the industry.

This is because there is only one producer and/or seller. Therefore, the firm's demand curve is the industry's demand curve. Since there are several buyers, an individual buyer cannot affect the price in a monopoly market.

2. **No close substitute**

In a monopoly, the product that the monopolist produces has no close substitute. If a close substitute exists, then the monopoly cannot exist.

Remember, a monopoly can only exist when the cross-elasticity of the product that the monopolist produces is zero. Therefore, the monopolist can determine the price of his own choice and refuse to sell below the determined price.

It is important to note that in real life, complete monopoly is extremely rare. However, one firm can dominate the supply of a good or a group of goods. For example, in public utilities, like transport, water, electricity, etc., monopolistic markets usually exist to reap the benefits of large-scale production.

3. **Strong barriers to the entry of new firms**

Even if the monopolist firm is earning super-normal profits, new firms face many hurdles in trying to enter the industry. There are many reasons for this like legal barriers, technology, or a naturally occurring substance which others cannot find. Sometimes, the monopolist works in a small market making it economically challenging for new firms to enter.

4. **Price Maker**

Since there is only one firm selling the product, it becomes the price maker for the whole industry. The consumers have to accept the price set by the firm as there are no other sellers or close substitutes.

A monopolistic firm is a price-maker, not a price-taker. Therefore, a monopolist can increase or decrease the price. Also, when the price changes, the average revenue, and marginal revenue changes too.

5. **Monopoly is also an Industry:**

Under monopoly there is only one firm which constitutes the industry. Difference between firm and industry comes to an end.

Monopolist has full control over the supply of commodity. Having control over the supply of the commodity he possesses the market power to set the price. Thus, as a single seller, monopolist may be a king without a crown. If there is to be monopoly, the cross elasticity of demand between the product of the monopolist and the product of any other seller must be very small.

- **Monopolistic Competition**

Meaning:

Monopolistic competition is a type of market structure where many companies are present in an industry, and they produce similar but differentiated products. None of the companies enjoy a monopoly, and each company operates independently without regard to the actions of other companies. The market structure is a form of imperfect competition.

The theory was developed almost simultaneously by the American economist Edward Hastings Chamberlin in his Theory of Monopolistic Competition (1933) and by the British economist Joan Robinson in her Economics of Imperfect Competition (1933).

Companies in a monopolistic competition make economic profits in the short run, but in the long run, they make zero economic profit. The latter is also a result of the freedom of entry and exit in the industry. Economic profits that exist in the short run attract new entries, which eventually lead to increased competition, lower prices, and high output.

Such a scenario inevitably eliminates economic profit and gradually leads to economic losses in the short run. The freedom to exit due to continued economic losses leads to an increase in prices and profits, which eliminates economic losses.

Unlike in perfect competition, firms that are monopolistically competitive maintain spare capacity. Models of monopolistic competition are often used to model industries. Textbook examples of industries with market structures similar to monopolistic competition include restaurants, cereal, clothing, shoes, and service industries in large cities.

Monopolistic competition is different from a monopoly. A monopoly exists when a person or entity is the exclusive supplier of a good or service in a market. The demand is inelastic and the market is inefficient.

Characteristics of Monopolistic Competition

Consider some of the characteristics of monopolistic competition.

1. **A large number of firms**: In this type of imperfect market, several firms compete for a market share with no single firm monopolizing the market.
2. **Product differentiation**: In monopolistic competition, each firm produces goods or services that are close substitutes for the goods or services produced by other firms. Competitive firms differentiate their similar products with distinct marketing strategies, brand names, and slightly different quality levels. Product differentiation enables firms to

command higher prices for lower quantities of goods.

3. **Low barriers to entry**: In a monopolistic market, new firms have low barriers to enter the market. Entrants can also exit the market with relative ease.
4. **Pricing**: Existing firms within this type of imperfect competition act as price makers and set prices for goods and services. Firms in monopolistic competition can lower prices without inciting a price war, a common problem in oligopolies. When marginal revenue equals marginal cost, firms in a monopolistic market achieve profit maximization. As more firms enter a market, the elasticity of the demand curve increases, making the quantities of a product sold more responsive to a price change.

Example of Monopolistic Competition

Monopolistic competition is a form of competition that characterizes a number of industries that are familiar to consumers in their day-to-day lives. Examples include restaurants, hair salons, clothing, and consumer electronics. To illustrate the characteristics of monopolistic competition, we'll use the example of household cleaning products.

Competing Companies

Say you've just moved into a new house and want to stock up on cleaning supplies. Go to the appropriate aisle in a grocery store, and you'll see that any given item—dish soap, hand soap, laundry detergent, surface disinfectant, toilet bowl cleaner, etc.—is available in a number of varieties. For each purchase you need to make, perhaps five or six firms will be competing for your business.

Product Differentiation

Because the products all serve the same purpose, there are relatively few options for sellers to differentiate their offerings from other competing firms. There might be "discount" varieties that are of lower quality, but it is difficult to tell whether the higher-priced options are in fact any better. This uncertainty results from imperfect information: the average consumer does not know the precise differences between the various products, or what the fair price for any of them is.

Monopolistic competition tends to lead to heavy marketing because different firms need to distinguish broadly similar products. One company might opt to lower the price of their cleaning product, sacrificing a higher profit margin in exchange—ideally—for higher sales. Another might take the opposite route, raising the price and using packaging that suggests quality and sophistication.

A third might sell itself as more eco-friendly, using "green" imagery and displaying a stamp of approval from an environmental certifier. In reality, every one of the brands might be equally effective.

Hair salons, restaurants, clothing, and consumer electronics are all examples of industries with monopolistic competition. Each company offers products that are similar to others in the same industry. However, they can distinguish themselves through marketing and branding.

Special Considerations

Firms in monopolistic competition face a significantly different business environment than those in either a monopoly or perfect competition. In addition to competing to reduce costs or scaling up production, companies in monopolistic competition can also distinguish themselves through other means.

Decision-Making

Monopolistic competition implies that there are enough firms in the industry so that one firm's decision does not require other companies to change their behavior. In an oligopoly, a price cut by one firm can set off a price war, but this is not the case for monopolistic competition.

Pricing Power

As in a monopoly, firms in monopolistic competition are price setters or makers, rather than price takers. However, their nominal ability to set prices is effectively offset by the fact that demand for their products is highly price-elastic. In order to actually raise their prices, the firms must be able to differentiate their products from those of their competitors by increasing their quality, real or perceived.

Demand Elasticity

Due to the range of similar offerings, demand is highly elastic in monopolistic competition. In other words, demand is very responsive to price changes. If your favorite multipurpose surface cleaner suddenly costs 20% more, you probably won't hesitate to switch to an alternative, and your countertops probably won't know the difference.

Economic Profit

In the short run, firms can make excess economic profits. However, because barriers to entry are low, other firms have an incentive to enter the market, increasing the competition, until overall economic profit is zero. Note that economic profits are not the same as accounting profits; a firm that posts a positive net income can have zero economic profit because the latter incorporates opportunity costs.

The long-run characteristics of a monopolistically competitive market are almost the same as a perfectly competitive market. Two differences between the two are that monopolistic competition produces heterogeneous products and that monopolistic competition involves a great deal of non-price competition, which is based on subtle product differentiation. A firm making profits in the short run will nonetheless only break even in the long run because demand will decrease and average total cost will increase. This means in the long run, a monopolistically competitive firm will make zero economic profit. This illustrates the amount of influence the firm has over the market; because of brand loyalty, it can raise its prices without losing all of its customers. This means that an individual firm's demand curve is downward sloping, in contrast to perfect competition, which has a perfectly elastic demand schedule.

Evidence suggests that consumers use information obtained from advertising not only to assess the single brand advertised, but also to infer the possible existence of brands that the consumer has, heretofore, not observed, as well as to infer consumer satisfaction with brands similar to the advertised brand.

References

-

•••

- https://www.yourarticlelibrary.com/foreign-trade/8-major-limitations-of-foreign-trade-322-words/5912
- https://www.investopedia.com/insights/what-is-international-trade/
- https://en.m.wikipedia.org/wiki/Foreign_trade_of_India
- http://www.simplynotes.in/uncategorized/trading-environment-of-international-trade/
- https://www.bing.com/images/search?q=international+trade&form=HDRSC2&first=1&tsc=ImageBasicHover
- https://www.geektonight.com/demand-function/
- https://www.thebalance.com/five-determinants-of-demand-with-examples-and-formula-3305706
- https://www.econlib.org/library/Topics/College/elasticityofdemand.html
- https://smallbusiness.chron.com/demand-forecasting-estimation-32783.html
- https://keydifferences.com/difference-between-short-run-and-long-run-production-function.html
- https://courses.lumenlearning.com/boundless-economics/chapter/the-production-function/
- https://www.economicsdiscussion.net/production-function/production-function-meaning-definitions-and-features/6892
- https://www.investopedia.com/terms/m/macroeconomics.asp
- https://www.tutorialspoint.com/managerial_economics/macroeconomics_basics.htm
- https://www.economicsdiscussion.net/macroeconomics/top-9-importance-of-macroeconomics-discussed/7569
- https://study.com/academy/lesson/what-is-economic-growth-and-development-definition-theories-indicators.html
- https://www.yourarticlelibrary.com/economics/3-important-methods-for-measuring-national-income/2792
- https://www.financialexpress.com/what-is/inflation-meaning/1618981/

- https://www.economicsdiscussion.net/inflation/theories-of-inflation/top-3-theories-of-inflation-with-diagram-2/8137
- https://www.vedantu.com/commerce/control-of-inflation
- https://study.com/academy/lesson/law-of-diminishing-returns-definition-examples-quiz.html
- https://personalexcellence.co/blog/diminishing-returns/
- https://egyankosh.ac.in/bitstream/123456789/22872/1/Unit-5.pdf
- https://www.economicsdiscussion.net/theory-of-cost/the-traditional-theory-of-costs-with-diagram/5160
- https://www.gacbe.ac.in/pdf/ematerial/18MEC11C-U4.pdf
- https://commerceiets.com/modern-theory-of-cost/
- https://www.toppr.com/guides/business-economics-cs/analysis-of-market/monopoly/
- https://corporatefinanceinstitute.com/resources/knowledge/economics/monopolistic-competition-2/
- https://www.cheggindia.com/career-guidance/managerial-economics-principals-types-and-scope/
- https://commercemates.com/role-and-importance-of-managerial-economics/
- https://theintactone.com/2019/10/13/me-u1-topic-2-managerial-economics-and-relationship-with-other-disciplines/
- https://www.slideshare.net/RichardAtusayeNgosi/role-of-managerial-economics-in-decision-making
- https://theintactone.com/2019/08/11/me-u1-topic-5-fundamental-principles-of-managerial-economics-incremental-principle-marginal-principle-opportunity-cost-principle-discounting-principle-concept-of-time-perspective-principle-equi/
- https://byjus.com/commerce/production-possibility-curve/
- https://www.vedantu.com/commerce/difference-between-cardinal-and-ordinal-utility
- https://corporatefinanceinstitute.com/resources/knowledge/economics/law-of-diminishing-marginal-utility/
- https://www.toppr.com/guides/business-economics/theory-of-consumer-behavior/indifference-curve/

Printed by Libri Plureos GmbH in Hamburg,
Germany